JOHNNY CASH

JOHNNY CASH
THE LAST INTERVIEW
and OTHER CONVERSATIONS

MELVILLE HOUSE
BROOKLYN · LONDON

Melville House Publishing   Suite 2000
         46 John Street   and   16/18 Woodford Road
Brooklyn, NY 11201   London E7 0HA

mhpbooks.com
@melvillehouse

ISBN: 978-1-61219-893-4
ISBN: 978-1-61219-894-1 (eBook)

Printed in the United States of America

1   3   5   7   9   10   8   6   4   2

A catalog record for this book is available from the Library of Congress.

CONTENTS

INTRODUCTION

PETER GURALNICK

"I'll bet I was the first person in this room who ever actually heard Robert Johnson!"

The speaker is Johnny Cash, who leaps up from his seat in the Grand Ballroom of the Waldorf Astoria on the occasion of his induction into the Rock & Roll Hall of Fame in 1992 to inform me of two things. First, this was his way of saying, in his customary good-humored and good-natured fashion, that he knew who I was. (I had published a book on Robert Johnson not too long ago.) But it was also his way of declaring, with a characteristic burst of enthusiasm, his all-out, all-consuming dedication to the music. And you know what? Surrounded though he was by rock critics and sober-minded scholars of the music, he may well have been right.

That dedication to the music, to music of all sorts, was one of his principal reasons for signing with Columbia Records in 1958, after first making his indelible mark on the tiny Sun label of Memphis with such epochal songs as "I Walk the Line," "Folsom Prison Blues," and "Big River"—and, in the process, derevolutionizing country music with his spare, and unsparingly honest, cut-down sound.

"There were so many things I wanted to do," he said of the switch to a major label. "I had all these ideas about special projects—different album ventures like *Ride This Train*, *From Sea to Shining Sea*, the Indian album—but I felt like at Sun I would be limited in what I could do, where with Columbia I could do all that and reach more people with my music." He was determined, he said, to expand his horizons. He wanted to explore the full range of his musical interests, not just with recapitulations of what he had already done but with musical expeditions that set off in other directions, both old and new. And over the years that is exactly what he did, always going back to the true sources: Sister Rosetta Tharpe, for example, for gospel; fabled Texas folklorist and historian J. Frank Dobie for authentic gunfighter ballads; songwriter Peter LaFarge, whom John and Pete Seeger speak fondly of in a 1966 television interview included here, for his groundbreaking album *Bitter Tears: Johnny Cash Sings Ballads of the American Indian*. And, well, Robert Johnson for the blues, whom he was introduced to shortly after his Columbia signing, when Don Law—the man who had signed him but had also recorded Robert Johnson some twenty years earlier, not long before the young bluesman's death—played him the tapes of Johnson's brilliant recordings well before the first earthshaking album of his songs, *Robert Johnson: King of the Delta Blues Singers*, introduced Robert Johnson to the world.

Only those who were there at the beginning, declared Sun session guitarist Roland Janes (he's the one soloing so brilliantly on all those Jerry Lee Lewis records), can understand how different Johnny Cash really was. The records, when they first started coming out on Sun in 1955, in the immediate wake of Elvis Presley's success, sounded "so unusual that I never would have dreamed he could have even gotten a record played on the radio. But he set country music on its ear." He was, in fact, so much of an outsider, he told Patrick Carr in a 1976 *Country Music* interview, included in these pages, that he was kept waiting for two hours in Grand Ole Opry manager Jim Denny's office before his Opry debut, and then he was asked, "What makes you think you belong on the Grand Ole Opry?" And this with a number-one hit on the country charts.

It was the voice that compelled attention from the start. It was a voice that Sun Records founder Sam Phillips compared to blues singer Howlin' Wolf's in its uniqueness, the unimpeachable integrity and originality of its sound—but it was the conviction *behind* the voice which allowed him to create a body of work as ambitious in its scope as it was homespun in its sound. And it was his unwavering insistence on an emotional truth that defied formulization, the restless probing of a mind that from childhood on was never satisfied with easy answers or ready-made solutions, that sustained a career of unflagging pursuit not so much of *the* truth (I don't think John would ever have been satisfied with that) as the multifarious *nature* of truth right up to the end of his life.

He grew up in the federal colony of Dyess, Arkansas, "a social experiment with a socialist setup, really," as Cash described it, "that was [established] by President Roosevelt for farmers that had lost out during the Depression." It was an experience that, far from being lost on the boy, underscored a dedication to community and social justice that remained with him all his life. And it offered opportunities that he recognized might otherwise never have come his way. One of his most vivid memories of Dyess was the day that Eleanor Roosevelt came to town to dedicate the library, a momentous occasion not simply for the glimpse it afforded of Mrs. Roosevelt but for the opportunity it subsequently provided him to indulge in what would become his lifelong passion for reading. "Well, you know, I always have been a bookworm. We had a very big library in Dyess—our library was maybe the biggest library in the state, and I got into just about everything. I can remember reading *Drums Along the Mohawk* and *The Last of the Mohicans*; I read all the Indian books I could get." And he read them not so much to escape, really, but with a voracity for discovery that would carry him out into a world that, in the absence of reading, he might never have been able to imagine, and long past the point, material and spiritual, that most people would gladly have embraced as the definition of success.

Music was always an integral part of his life. "My parents woke me up every morning with the radio on playing country music." When he was sixteen and still a high tenor, John's mother, Carrie, paid for voice lessons for her son because she sensed a potential in this boy who was always singing "Irish ballads, Bill Monroe bluegrass songs, I knew 'Don't Sit Under the Apple Tree with Anyone Else But Me' as well as 'Rainbow at Midnight,' I wasn't locked into any one kind of music. In my mind I didn't separate the songs, I loved all kinds of music when I was a kid, and I wasn't conscious of any separation."

It was this sense of the limitlessness of music that bound him most closely to his discoverer (and Elvis's and Jerry Lee Lewis's), Sam Phillips. "He told me, when 'I Walk the Line' hit—he didn't say much until then—he said, 'Now you see what I'm talking about. The record has crossed over out of the country into the pop. Now your country music can no longer be locked into any one category.' He said, 'That's what music is all about. It should be universal.' And I said, 'Well, Sam, that's what I've always believed, too.'"

Even at his lowest ebb, in the years during which, by virtue of his admittedly self-destructive, drug-dependent behavior, John Cash should have been lost to the world, some of his most worthwhile projects still emerged (*Bitter Tears*, for example, came out in 1964, *Orange Blossom Special* in 1965), outgrowths of the same restless intelligence that, in the last decade of his life, prompted him to take a chance on making records with hip-hop producer Rick Rubin and make albums, *contemporary* albums, that reflected both the darkest depths and some of the highest spirits of his musical career. He never rejected the human impulse that led to his longtime addiction to amphetamines; he never pretended to be anything but what he was. "I've talked to those pills," he would say, even in his later years. "I want to take amphetamines right now," he declared in a 1988 interview, long after his spiritual redemption and religious reawakening were thought to have removed him from temptation. It might have made his public feel better to hear him declare outright victory, but he never failed to address the subject with the same unsparing honesty that he brought to all of his endeavors, musical, intellectual, and emotional. Much as he embraced, and constantly cited, the lyrics of Kris Kristofferson's "The Pilgrim, Chapter 33," which he said Kristofferson had written for him ("He's a walkin' contradiction, partly truth and partly fiction"), to help explain something of his belief that we are *all* the sum of our inescapably contradictory parts.

He retained his ingenuous sense of wonder, his keen analytic gift, and his taste for uncharted adventure to the end. He could be as excited and passionate sometimes about ideas that didn't work out, as things that did. He was constant in so many, many ways, but at the same time he was never anything less than surprising. He may have been the only one of the Sun rockabillies to sing about plowing behind a mule. He was also the only one who would dare to sing the songs of another, far-removed generation and find a new audience for the raw honesty of his music with songs by groups like Soundgarden and Nine Inch Nails. I asked him one time if he ever worried about outrunning his audience. "You know, I've thought about that," he said, with what I took to be a certain amount of calculation. "I've been careful about that. I don't think I'd ever get ahead of my audience. If I ever feel like I might have, with my fancy suit and my eight-piece band, I'll just tell five of them to be quiet, take the other three, and do 'Give My Love to Rose.'"

Seeing him perform was almost like getting a lesson in American history—and not just American *musical* history either. The first time I saw Johnny Cash in person, at the Boston Arena in 1964, Mother Maybelle Carter and the Carter Sisters (including his future wife-to-be, June) were on the bill, along with fifties country music superstar Webb Pierce (eleven number one hits in the first half of the decade alone), and fifteen-year-old Hank Williams Jr., who imparted his own teenage twist to his father's iconic songs. Along with John's own wide-ranging repertoire, that pretty much carried you from the beginning right up to the present moment in country music history. But then (as if that weren't enough), as we emerged in somewhat dazed fashion from the crumbling, all-purpose serviceability of the Boston Arena, we were confronted by the gleaming splendor of Webb Pierce's 1962 Pontiac Bonneville, decked out with more than 150 silver dollars, a pair of steer horns mounted across the front grille, and ornamental artillery (six-shooters and rifles) mounted front and rear. Which, like the music, served in its own way as a portal to yet another world.

John remained a dedicated scholar and song catcher, always. Like both Elvis and Jerry Lee Lewis, he was a passionate archivist—though he may have pursued it in somewhat more systematic fashion. One time his daughter Rosanne, an equally dedicated songwriter and performer, in whom he inculcated not only his love of music but his own stubborn sense of independence, was digging into the origins of the music and called him up to ask "about the old songs. I asked about songs about mothers, babies, brothers and sisters, fathers and grandparents," she wrote. "He gave me titles, years and the names of the recording artists, and then sang them to me over the phone, verse by verse, more excited by each new recollection. 'I know all of them!' he said happily," and then told her to call him back the next morning so they could talk about the music some more.

When she did, he announced to her, "'There's a whole other group of songs, if you're interested.' 'About who?' I asked. 'Dead dogs,' he answered, solemnly, and rattled off a list of titles. I laughed," she wrote, but in a sense, she recognized, it was no laughing matter. Music was, she had come to realize, as much as anything what bound them together, the very thing that, as nearly everyone I've ever written about, from Sam Phillips to Solomon Burke to . . . *Johnny Cash*, has affirmed, has the potential to bind us *all* together, perhaps the one place where "the longing to connect," in Rosanne's words, can be "completely satisfied."

William Faulkner found in his own "little postage stamp of native soil" an inexhaustible source of inspiration. The same could be said of Johnny Cash. If you were unafraid to explore the emotional terrain that was offered you, there was no end to the breadth of emotional truth that you could deliver. There was, as John often remarked, no safe harbor for the creative soul. He was tormented by demons that he could not always control, but he never sought excuses. "I wouldn't let anybody influence me into thinking I was doing the wrong thing by singing about death, hell, and drugs," he says defiantly in his last interview with MTV's Kurt Loder. "'Cause I've always done that, and I always will."

This is what gives his music, at the same time, such breadth and specificity. Through imagination he had been granted the gift of empathetic transference, and he never turned away from it; unlike many artists, he was able to take on other voices and make them his own. His music celebrated the power of the individual human spirit, but his emphasis on directness and simplicity made a complex, and sometimes contradictory, message accessible to all. "Ride this train!" he called out, echoing Sister Rosetta Tharpe's more explicit spiritual invitation ("This train is bound for glory") with no less spiritual a message of his own. And there was never a moment in his life when he gave any evidence that he was tempted to get off that train.

JOHNNY CASH

"TAKE YOUR SHOES OFF"

INTERVIEW BY PETE SEEGER
RAINBOW QUEST
1966

[Seeger plays "Sinking in the Lonesome Sea"]

PETE SEEGER: That song, when I heard it first, had two people singing the chorus; they got lovely harmony. And uh, that was twenty-five years ago, but I'll never forget that record. And I don't think I'll ever forget the record I heard of a song, *[sings]* "You gotta walk that lonesome valley," or the song, "John Hardy was a desperate little man," or about two, three, four dozen other songs. And the reason I won't forget 'em is the same reason that millions of other Americans won't forget 'em. It was wonderful music made by a group called the Carter Family: old A. P. Carter from Virginia, and his daughter Maybelle, and his sister Sara, and um . . .

Way back round the early 1930s, you coulda heard their records on all kinds of country music programs around this country, north and south, and me, I was just one of millions that thought it was the most wonderful music I heard. Well, I sing it by way of introducing the person who's gonna be on our program, this rainbow quest today, who's come around, we're very fortunate to have Mother Maybelle's daughter, June Carter. She's traveling through town, and she said she might drop over and sing a few songs with us. And with her is another fellow. Well, let me tell you a little bit about him too, because he's kind of interesting.

You know, people like me up north, we sang songs about what it was like to be a farmer down south like . . . [*sings*] "Seven cent cotton and forty cent meat, how in the world can a poor man eat? Flower up high and cotton down low, how in the world can we raise the dough?" But coming out of my mouth, a song like that sounded kinda funny, and silly. I was never a cotton farmer, I never walked behind a mule. Never drove a truck either, except just my own little pickup truck. This fellow who's gonna drop around to our program, in just a few minutes you'll meet him, came out of a family of hard-working people in Arkansas, and a lot of hard work himself. But he also liked to pick a guitar, he liked to make up songs, and his songs touch the heartstrings of all kinds of people around the country.

Back in the era of the 1950s, maybe you remember them. [*sings*] "I'll walk the line . . ." and a whole bunch of other ones. But instead of me talking about him, I think you ought to meet him yourself. His name is Johnny Cash. Now of course, he and June Carter and some other musicians, they've been touring around the world. They just got back from overseas, a whole big show. And normally, it's a little unfair to ask them to perform without their whole show here, because it's a wonderful show, but I asked them to come around just the two of them, so we can get a chance to talk a little, and uh, if we kind of improvise our way through a program, I think maybe you'll get to know 'em better. It won't be an act or anything like that, because they're singing songs that they believe in and they feel. June Carter and Johnny Cash, just a moment.

[*Cash sings "I Am a Pilgrim"*]

SEEGER: Oh Johnny, you know, you know so many thousands of different songs. I know we're not gonna get time to do more than a few of 'em on this program. I hope you sing a couple that you've made up and a couple old ones.

JOHNNY CASH: Well, thank you Pete, I'd love to. That song there, that is the first time I think I ever sang that song [*unintelligible*], thanks to June Carter and yourself.

JUNE CARTER: You missed your note, Pete, he gave you a break all of your own and you missed it.

CASH: Best to let the people know that Pete's coming in.

SEEGER: Yeah, well, June, what are you doing with a banjo in your hand?

CARTER: I'm holding it. [*laughs*] No, Pete, I tell ya, I'm not a banjo player, especially around you. I've listened to you play for so many years, I pluck on one a little bit sometime, and listen to my mother play the old drop thumb lick. And I've listened to good banjo players, and that's about as close as I am to being a banjo player, I just hit a lick here and there.

CASH: Yeah, she's a clever thief . . . you know, picking up the licks. No she's very good, Pete, I'm very proud of her. In Korea, we went for the armed forces, Korea, Japan, and all of the Far East, about three years ago, and it's the first tour she ever played the banjo on, and the troops just loved her for it.

CARTER: I had to, I didn't have a front tooth! That's a story all its own, would you like to hear it? We were playing at a place back up in Korea called Camp Howard, way away from way back up in behind Seoul up there in the mountains, and so many of the boys hadn't been home in so long, you know, and they hadn't seen an American girl I don't know when. And I'm in there with a whole mouthful of teeth and grinning and smiling. I do the first tune on the stage, and I had this cute little trick where I used to take the microphone and sing this little song, and throw the mic into the footlights and yank it back real quick. Well, it always came back. And that day, it really came back. It hit me right in the mouth and knocked teeth everywhere. And I'm standing there with my head down and my teeth, I'm picking 'em up off the floor, and I didn't know what to do, I didn't know whether to sing, cry, or what to do.

At any rate, I sang, with my teeth out. Because they were lined up for like miles to get to the show, and I thought well, even without a tooth, I think maybe they'd like to hear a good old girl from home. So I stood up there and propped my foot on that chair and picked the banjo, and picked a guitar, and just grinned like I had a tooth.

CASH: That's the way that, uh, she came downstairs for breakfast at Seoul, Korea, and she's so homesick I guess, or she was thinking about home, she says first thing, she says, "I know where there's a whole bunch of huckleberries." And I said, uh—

CARTER: It wasn't in Korea.

CASH: I said, "Where's that, June?" Yes it was, in Seoul, Korea.

CARTER: Yeah, but that wasn't where the huckleberries were.

CASH: I know, but I said, "Where's that, June?" She says, "Well, you know where Grandma Carter lives? Well, go over the knob, and then go up Clinton Mountain about two hundred feet, and there's a whole bunch of huckleberries.

CARTER: It was about that time for the huckleberries.

CASH: Nobody said a word.

CARTER: I was wanting some huckleberries. And, uh, speaking of Grandma Carter, Pete, you were talking about the Carter Family a minute ago, and I'm afraid you're just a little bit confused about something. Do you mind if I tell you the whole story?

SEEGER: Will you set me straight?

CARTER: All right. Well, there was the old original Carter Family, A. P., Sara, and Maybelle, that you know. But you've got their relationships mixed up a bit.

SEEGER: Wasn't Maybelle A. P.'s daughter?

CARTER: No, she was A. P.'s sister-in-law. She's my daddy's wife, and he was A. P.'s brother, and Aunt Sara was not his sister, but his wife. And she and mother were first cousins, so that makes you your own grandpa.

CASH: One thing here, June, real quick: Aunt Sara Carter is coming to Nashville; she's there today, she arrived today. For the first time in twenty years, I suppose, Sara Carter is going to record, with Maybelle. The two of them, just the two of them. And this should be a real collector's item; she sings great.

CARTER: Well, this is the first time that mother and Aunt Sara, they cut their last recording in 1941, and you see A. P.'s been dead quite a while —

CASH: Twenty-five.

CARTER: —Well, I said, I mean the last recording, excuse me; he's been gone quite a while. And that's all of the old original sound that's left, mother and Aunt Sara. We're real happy about it. Um, she just didn't have anything to do with the music business, she really didn't care, you know, too much. Except, we got to sending her tapes, talking to her, and she got to sending us tapes of her, of songs she had sung. And she has the greatest voice, Pete, it's just as strong and vibrant as it can be. And she sent cold chills all over us with those old tapes she sent, so John and Mommy and Daddy and the girls and I sent her a tape and begged her to come. So she's coming!

SEEGER: Oh, wonderful.

CARTER: And we're just thrilled to death about it.

CASH: It'll be a, I think, a real collector's item. Uh, Sara and Maybelle Carter, singing the old songs, their style, nobody else in the background, you know? Pure, she's as pure as the driven snow, or her voice is, anyway, I don't know much about her background. June probably does. But she is a great lady, and a fabulous—she got a fabulous voice.

SEEGER: Oh, what would be one of those songs we can sing together?

CARTER: You mean an old Carter Family song?

SEEGER: Whatever you want.

CARTER: Well, do you have any preference? Do you ever sing "The Worried Man Blues?"

SEEGER: Oh, I sing it all the time.

CARTER: Do you really? Well, we could try that one.

SEEGER: If you lead off on it, though, because I—

CARTER: I don't know if I can pick that on a banjo or not. John, do you mind giving me the guitar?

CASH: No.

CARTER: Well, I'll take that, and we can take it from there, and see where we go. Going way back on this one.

[*Carter and Seeger play "The Worried Man Blues"*]

CARTER: [*laughs*] Oh, that was fun!

CASH: My favorite's "Keep on the Sunny Side." June and Marshall Grant, my bass player, and I do this on stage sometime. [*June and Pete sing a lyric*] I'll tell ya, real quickly, a story of why this song impressed me so. June asked me to go up to see her old home place up at Maces Springs, Virginia, you know where that is, of course. Maces Springs, that's near Hiltons. Uh, anyway, at uh—what's the name of the cemetery?

CARTER: Mount Vernon.

CASH: Mount Vernon cemetery, we drove up this winding gravel road, and the tall pines all the way around, and there was one little spot of sunlight, way down at the end, and the sun was shining on a rose marble monument. Well, we walked right straight to it, and the writing was on the other side. And I said, "That's it, June." She'd never seen it either—she'd heard about it, she knew about it. I walked around, and uh, right where the sun was streaming down, um, on this rose marble, the words said A. P. CARTER, and a gold record under that, and under that, KEEP ON THE SUNNY SIDE. And he was on the sunny side. They buried him where the sun would shine on him, it seen more hours of the day than anywhere else.

CARTER: Did you ever know him, Pete?

SEEGER: No, just heard his records, that's all.

CARTER: Well, do you know, would you let me tell you a little something about him?

SEEGER: Yeah, please.

CASH: I will, too.

CARTER: Well, my uncle A. P. Carter, 'course that's my daddy's brother, he was a tall man, he was about six-two and a half, six-three, something like that. He was quite tall, and he was quite handsome when he was young. Dark, and I mean, you know, darker hair, and some of the people may have seen his pictures, I don't know. But he walked like a giant; I don't know how to justify that other than the fact that when he walked onto a stage, years and years ago, the old Carter Family did concerts without even realizing that they did. He walked out on that stage, and there was something about that man that just demanded attention and got it. He stood, and mother and Aunt Sara used to sit down with their guitars, and the old lamps would be lined across the front of the stage.

CASH: No microphones.

CARTER: No mics, at all. But he would tell a story about the songs: where he got it, where it came from, if they wrote it, or where he got the song, and how come them to do the song. And uh, so many of the particular songs they did, like the "Cyclone of Rye Cove," which was written about the disaster at the Rye Cove schoolhouse, he told why, where it came from, the "Fate of Dewey Lee," so many of those old ones. But the songs from the Spanish-American War and things like that, he would just say he got this down on the river, you know, such-and-such's house, but where it came from, you know?

And um, there was just something about the man that made him great. And mother and Aunt Sara had the same thing, I don't know what it was, but it just demanded respect; they got it. And the country people used to come and listen to them, and I remember one story that was told by Mr. J. L. Franks, who used to do all of the shows from out of the Grand Ole Opry, he said, "Without the Carter Family, we might have gone under." He said—now this is years ago, you know—he said that when Pee Wee King and Eddie Arnold and all of 'em, Minnie Pearl started from the Grand Ole Opry, they'd play tours, and he said, "We'd go out and do enough to barely get by. And then we'd be starving," and then he'd say, "I'll have to see if I can just get a hold of A. P. Carter." And he said they called somebody at Hilton's, and somebody'd go up the valley, and they'd leave that mountain there and come out, and he said, "Then we'd have a whole week of good dates if we could just get the Carter Family." And so that's the way it was back then. But he was quite a man.

SEEGER: It's this tradition, you know, of singing the old songs and then also making up new ones, which is the wonderful thing which the Carter Family taught to me and many other people. Woody Guthrie got it from them. The idea that folk music wasn't just old music, it wasn't just new music; it was a combination of the old and new, all mixed up together. And no two people sang 'em exactly the same. That's the wonderful thing about it, that you get hold of an old song and you kind of wear it a little bit until, finally, after you've sung it a few years, it's like a good old pair of shoes; it just fits your feet. Johnny, I want you to sing some of your songs, too. Uh, just a moment though, we got an interruption here, but we'll be back in a second.

[*commercial break*]

CASH: [*Cash has removed his shoes*] Pete, when I was a kid— say one, two, three, four, five years old—my dad hopped freight trains, rode the rods, the boxcars, on top of 'em, to wherever he could get work, you know. He always sent the money back home, and that left, except for the kids in school, my mother and I. She played the guitar, and she has a [*strums*] that lick there. And I just loved it. And the first song I ever learned was one that she sang. She might've been thinking about my dad, who was away, working for a living, sending money home, when she sang, so often, "There's a mother always waiting you at home." That's the very first song I remember.

CARTER: Why don't you sing it?

[Cash plays "There's a Mother Always Waiting You at Home]

SEEGER: Was that back in the thirties, in Depression era?

CASH: I was born '32, so I'd guess '35, '36. Well, 1935, I remember my mother playing the guitar and singing.

SEEGER: When did you first start making up songs?

CASH: Just not long after that, but I hid them, and burned 'em, and threw 'em away, you know? But uh, the first one that I have kept, I was twelve years old, and I wrote poems, songs, short stories, and drew pictures, a little of everything, to keep my grades way down to C and D, until they clamped down on me. But uh, I went into the air force after I graduated from high school, and um, I was in Germany, in the air force, in the bitter winter in January. A blizzard was raging; I had five dollars in my pocket. I walked the five miles to Landsburg and bought a five-dollar German guitar. It had no name, but that's how I got my start. I was twenty-one. And uh, I'd written several, well countless songs up to then, but I had the tunes here, *[taps forehead]* you know?

SEEGER: You were singing one back there in the dressing room, one about the Mississippi flood, was it? 1937?

CASH: Oh, we were in that.

SEEGER: Sing just a little bit of that.

CASH: All right. [*strums*] My daddy sat on the front steps of the house and watched the water rising from the levee breaking. Five steps, and every day he'd say, "Well, it's over another step." And Momma'd say, "How high's the water?" And he'd say, "Well, it's two, three, four, five feet high and rising." When it was five, he had to get out. He swam to the road. [*sings*] "How high is the water, Momma?" I wrote this twenty-five years later. [*sings*] "Two feet high and rising." [*continues singing*]

[*Cash plays "Two Feet High and Rising"*]

CASH: That was '37. In '38 there was a good cotton crop, and picking time was real good.

SEEGER: Oh, sing that, then.

CASH: Oh, I'm sorry; I wasn't asking to do another song.

SEEGER: I want to hear it.

CASH: But it was, it was a bumper crop that year, and this, this song came from thinking about the crops in '38, '39, '40, '41, in the delta land in northeast Arkansas.

[*Cash plays "Pickin' Time"*]

CARTER: He always does. That's good.

CASH: Wait for [*unintelligible*] for picking time.

SEEGER: Johnny, you and I, and June too, we had a very dear friend who's not with us anymore, and uh, I'd like to sing a song of his. I don't know if you know—

CASH: You're talking about Peter La Farge.

SEEGER: Pete La Farge, Indian, and proud of it—

CASH: I am, too.

SEEGER: You're part Indian?

CASH: I'm proud of Peter. Yes, I'm part Cherokee.

SEEGER: No foolin'.

CASH: Peter was Hopi, I understand. Full-blooded Hopi.

SEEGER: Well, Pete came to New York; I met him about four, five years ago. He helped me build a chimney back at our house.

CASH: He told me about that.

CARTER: We saw the chimney.

SEEGER: Great big stone. I thought it was gonna break through the floor before we got it up.

CASH: He was a great man.

SEEGER: Well, he was a very thoughtful guy, and I think in many ways one of the most thoughtful people I knew. He told me how Indian people had a feeling for the world and nature that he found missing in a lot of city people. He told me about the little coyote, for example. As far as the ranches were concerned, they just want to poison him out of existence. But the Indians' name for the coyote was "Little Brother," and he had a song about it.

[Seeger plays "Coyote, My Little Brother"]

SEEGER: Kind of a wail, not a song. You get that out of the flat plains.

CASH: Yeah, in '57 I wrote a song called "Old Apache Squaw," and then forgot the Indian so-called protest for a while. Nobody else seemed to speak up with any volume or voice. Then, not long before I met Peter, I wrote a thing called "Apache Tears." You know, the stone out west, at the souvenir shops, that they smooth in a tumbler. It's black, it looks like a tear. I wrote a song called "Apache Tears," and I wrote one called "The Ballad of the Talking Leaves," the story of the creation of the Cherokee alphabet.

SEEGER: Hey, no foolin', I wanna learn that.

CASH: And—well, I'll give you seven hundred thousand copies of it. Anyway—

SEEGER: I just read about Sequoyah a few weeks ago.

CASH: Did you?

SEEGER: A tremendous guy. Without any formal education, he decided that the Cherokees should have their own written language, that they had to organize themselves if they were going to withstand the encroaching settlers.

CASH: In my album, there's a little story that tells how he came to do this. He was fifteen years old; he was following his father across a battlefield where they'd been fighting white men, and some officer's notebook had scattered in the wind—the pages. And Sequoyah had never seen paper. Never. Never seen printed word on paper. And he picked them up as he went along, and he ran up to his father and said, "What is this, father? These strange squares, with such beautiful bird track marks on them." He said, "Not even the owl could put these there." And his father grabbed them from him, said, "That's the white man's talking leaves." And he said, "Talking leaves, what do you mean?" And he said, "Just forget it." Well, he followed him, finally got it out of him. He said, "That is how they communicate. They make bird track marks on these snow white leaves, and they send it to their brother, and his brother knows what's in his heart, or what he's thinking." So I wrote the thing about—

SEEGER: About how Sequoyah made up the Cherokee alphabet.

CASH: Mm-hmm. Which is, as you know, the most complicated alphabet in, I suppose, in the history of the world. Something like seventy, eighty letters.

SEEGER: At the same time, it was so simple for Cherokees, that within a few weeks, a Cherokee boy could be writing letters to his own family. That's what I understood, that within three years, the entire Cherokee nation was reading and writing.

CASH: Right, because, I mean, they were a great, a noble race. And they said, the white man can talk on leaves, why not the Cherokee? And they studied it; it was pounded into their heads; they wanted to learn it and they did. And there's a newspaper published now, in Phoenix, in Cherokee.

SEEGER: Johnny, just a minute, I want you to sing one of these songs, either one of yours, or the one Pete wrote, telling the story of the American Indian people. Okay?

CASH: Yes, Peter La Farge was an Indian who loved his heritage, his country, and most of all—well, not most of all—but he did love his music. And he used it not as a vicious tool, but as a great, well, as a voice for the American Indian. And we were very proud that he came down from New York City and brought us five songs to do in this *Bitter Tears* album. Protest songs, for the American Indian, which I think was long overdue. Here's our favorite. June, would you have me on this one?

CARTER: Sure, and Pete too, you don't need—

CASH: Our favorite Peter La Farge Indian song.

[*Cash, Carter, and Seeger play "As Long as the Grass Shall Grow"*]

SEEGER: Johnny and June, I'm mighty glad that America has people like you traveling around, flying around. I know you keep on the run more than almost anybody I know. Every time I see you, you're just kind of zipping through. Let me sing a song for you both, as you fly around. [*tunes instrument*] One of my favorite old banjo tunes, I don't know if you heard it before.

CASH: After you do this one, would you do me a special request? We came to New York just to get you to do this special request. Would you play just a little bit of "Cripple Creek" on the fretless banjo?

SEEGER: All right.

CASH: Go right ahead, Pete.

[*Seeger plays "Little Birdy"*]

CASH: I wish I could do that, but you know I picked cotton for so many years, and uh, that's a different lick, picking cotton.

SEEGER: You want me to do something on the fretless banjo?

CASH: If you don't mind, I'd love to hear you.

SEEGER: Well, listen, the banjo you gave me, Bob Johnson gave it to you, and you brought it up to me, and uh—

CASH: 1855, that's older than June.

CARTER: [*unintelligible because Seeger's already strumming*]

SEEGER: I'm afraid it's right in between the frets.

CARTER: Yeah, that's right.

[*Seeger plays "Cripple Creek," clapping*]

CARTER: That's good.

SEEGER: Uh, how many more minutes do we have, Mr. Mann? Four minutes more? I want June to sing a song: [*sings*] "I'm thinking tonight of my blue eyes."

CASH: That's beautiful—

CARTER: I've never sung it as many times as the Carter Family did, but I'd try for you, Pete, if you wanted to.

SEEGER: I might say, this song doesn't have but about two or three verses, but it's a lot of fun to sing—it's a lot of fun to harmonize on, too. Any of you out there, you know that the main reason for this *Rainbow Quest* show is not just to show what we can do, but to show you how you can have a lot of fun yourself, making music. I mean it. I hope that you all out there, young, old, tall, short, fat or thin, quick or slow, no matter what kind of color or shape of person you are, if you like to make music, why, go ahead. Don't let the microphones and loudspeakers faze you.

CASH: Take your shoes off.

SEEGER: [*laughs*] Right. And this would be a good song to try, if you want to. Have you got a D chord there, because you're D—

CASH: Uh, I have a small one.

SEEGER: It comes out the same as your C.

CARTER: I'm in C. Where are you, Pete?

SEEGER: Wait till I get in gear here.

CASH: I thought it was a D flat, but you gave me a D and I just flattened it myself.

CARTER: I take a while to tune. It's like mother Maybelle; she'd stop and tune if the world come to an end.

CASH: Well, she does get it tuned, and she plays it.

[*Carter and Seeger play "I'm Thinking Tonight of My Blue Eyes"*]

"CASH COMES BACK" / "JOHNNY CASH'S FREEDOM"

INTERVIEWS BY PATRICK CARR
COUNTRY MUSIC
1976, 1978

"CASH COMES BACK" (1976)

PATRICK CARR: When I interviewed you two years ago, you said, "It's apparent that what I've been doing is not really what the people want to hear, so I'm going to try to do something that they want to hear." It strikes me, after listening to the *One Piece at a Time* album, that you've done just that.

JOHNNY CASH: I meant what I said, see . . . right? I think that I did something they wanted to hear, and what they wanted to hear was what I've done best all along—and that's the three-chord ballad with the Tennessee Three. I'm glad that's what they want because I know how to do that.

CARR: Is that what you enjoy doing most?

CASH: Yes, it really is. It's what I enjoy most. I'm getting such a kick out of it, feeling the same things I was feeling twenty years ago in my music. It's a whole new discovery for me, y'know—like, "Hey, I remember how good this felt, and I remember when I did it like this, and this is the way it feels best." Y'know? I just recorded a song I wrote eighteen years ago and forgot about. A song called "It's All Over." It sounds like the things I was doing eighteen years ago, and that's the way I recorded it, with the Tennessee Three. It's a weeper, a love song. It's kind of like being reborn again. I started out with that old simple sound on Sun Records, and I enjoyed it, and the people enjoyed it. But then I went through kind of a period there. Y'know, the real problem was not that I wasn't enjoying what I was doing; it was just that I was looking for something new, seeing if there was a new way for me to do it. As it turns out, what I think I discovered was that the way I started with it, the old way I've always done it, is the way I really enjoy it. You'd feel the atmosphere in the studio now . . . There's a lot of laughter at my sessions. There's a lot of horsing around, joking, kidding each other. It used to be like pulling teeth, like "OK, let's get this over with." It's not that way anymore. It's joy, it's fun.

CARR: During that whole period when you were messing around with arrangements and so on, were you in control? Was all that stuff your doing?

CASH: Well, I agreed to it. That came out of a meeting I had with some Columbia Records people. They came out to my concert in Las Vegas, and they talked about "Let's try something. Let's try this arranged. Let's try recording with the Big Sound. "

CARR: Was the arranger Gary Klein?

CASH: Yes. For that kind of stuff, Gary is the best there is. He really knows what he's doing . . . They thought it was the way to go, and I didn't know for sure at the time. So I went along with it, and I let them select most of the songs—which was a mistake because if I'm not personally involved in my music, it ain't going to be right. I'm not going to have a feeling for it when I go into the studio. So all that whole scene, as capable as Gary Klein is, was a wrong scene for me. But I learned a lot, and somewhere along the line Gary and I will do something—something that requires the kind of taste and artistry he's got. But it's like, ah—please pardon me for getting into politics—it's like we learned from the Vietnam War not to send troops to Africa, y'know? [*laughs*] And by the same token, I learned from those production days with Gary Klein that I shouldn't do it that way anymore.

CARR: These days you're choosing your own material, right?

CASH: Yeah. That's the big thing, too. These days I'm totally involved with it from the time I choose the songs until the thing is finished in the mix. That's another thing I didn't use to get involved in. After the session was over, I'd never be there for the mix. I threw a lot of good sounds away because I didn't give 'em my ideas, y'know? Charlie Bragg works with me at the studio, and he's the one who harped on me about "Go back to the old sound, go back to the old sound." My attitude was "Oh, I can *always* do *that*. I want to do something else." So he mixed it the way I wanted him to. I'd tell him how I wanted it, and that's the way he'd do it—under protest. He was a mighty happy man when I got into the studio with him when he'd called a session for mixing, and I said, "Let's put the slapback on there. Let's put the old Sun slapback on there and forget about quadrophonic sound and stereo and everything, and make it sound like 1957." And I enjoyed it! I didn't think I'd enjoy it, but I did, and I got to thinking . . . "Cash, you got involved in selecting the song; you put it down the way you wanted it; you saw it through the session. It would be stupid now to stay out of the mixing—like getting a ship almost to the shore, then turning it over to somebody else in the middle of a storm." So now I go in with Charlie on the mixing, and I tell him how I want it. We have some disagreements, but it always comes out the way I want it. [*laughs*] I'm really enjoying it. I guess that's the whole key to it. If I don't enjoy it, somehow the people out there know it. For some reason, they know it.

CARR: Well, they usually do, don't they? That's what most of those producers forget. But how did you come by "One Piece at a Time," John?

CASH: Don Davis found it, and called me. Wayne Kemp was going to record it himself, but Don asked him to let me have it. They agreed, and Don brought it out to me.

CARR: Did you know it was the one when you heard it?

CASH: Yeah, I knew it. I knew that was it.

CARR: That's your first Number One single in . . . oh, how long now?

CASH: I guess since "Man In Black" . . . no, since "Flesh And

Blood," 1971. Five years.

CARR: It must feel kinda good.

CASH: It really does. It really does. It's a joy, y'know? I dunno, maybe it's 'cause I'm older now. I used to take those hit records for granted. Back when everything I was releasing was going to Number One or up in the tops, I kinda took it for granted. Like, I would never look at the trade magazines. People would say, "Congratulations on your Number One record," and I wouldn't even know it was Number One. But it's like everyone shared in the excitement of "One Piece at a Time" being Number One. Everybody in town would be calling the office or the studio, saying, "It's number seven this week," and somebody would get a tip that it was going to be number four next week, and they'd call. So I started looking at the trade magazines. I still don't read 'em, but I look at the charts and see who's doing what and what's happening in the business . . . who's selling, who's not. It's kinda interesting—again. See, I had a couple of side involvements that took a lot of time and energy—but those were awfully important to me, and they were what I wanted them to be. That was my movie and my book. And you've only got so much energy. Right now I'm putting my energy into my music.

CARR: What about Jack Clement? Anything doing there? Are you doing any work with him?

CASH: Well, Jack Clement is always around, and I feel like I am, too, and sooner or later Jack Clement and I will do something together again. We didn't do too bad on "Ring of Fire" and "Ballad of a Teenage Queen" and "Guess Things Happen That Way," some of those—and we'll have some ideas that gel perfectly sometimes, and we'll get back in the studio together eventually.

CARR: Is anything going to happen to those tracks you recorded with Clement and Wolf a couple of years ago—the first cut on "Committed to Parkview," "You're So Heavenly Minded," "You're No Earthly Good"—all those?

CASH: Ah . . . We had one that I really like, "Someday My Ship Will Sail." I think Waylon and I are going to get that one out and listen to it again and see if we need to do anything to it. Waylon and I just did another session, did you know that?

CARR: Yeah. Just this past Monday, right?

CASH: Yeah. We cut two tracks for a single together, "I Wish I Was Crazy Again" and "There Ain't No Good Chain Gang." I guess we're just going to call the record companies' bluff. They say we can't record an album together, but I think we're going to do it anyway, and then say, "Here it is, work something out." I guess we could both get in trouble, but I tell you what: I respect Waylon as an artist, and I think he respects me. We've been friends for fifteen years and we always did enjoy working together, and just because we both happen to be professionals and make a lot of money for other people doing it, I really don't see where that should hold us back artistically.

If we want to get back in the studio together, we're going to do it. I think these record companies ought to set up a subsidiary amongst them for people like us, 'cause we're going to cut an album together. No doubt. We might do some country classics like "Lost Highway," some of those old heavy things. And we'll do it.

CARR: You were talking about taking more control over your music. Did the *One Piece at a Time* album really satisfy you on that level?

CASH: No, it just kinda got me primed and cocked for more and better to come. Like, it slipped me back into a whole new world of music and directions . . . like, I just recorded an old Presley song, "I'm Left, You're Right, She's Gone," and I did it with trumpets like I had on "Ring of Fire," and I've kind of got a sneaky feeling about that one. I really like the sound of it. I've always loved the song . . . So we're going to do an album of the old Sun things, the old Memphis stuff—'53 to '56. That's my next album project, the second one after *One Piece at a Time*: some of my songs, a couple of Presley's, maybe a Carl Perkins song, a Roy Orbison song. It's not just an attempt to recreate that sound. I think we can make it sound like today's market, like today's thing, y'know? 'Cause I really enjoy it, and I search my conscience, and if I sing something I really enjoy, then that's what I ought to do. It's not always commercial, but it's what I ought to do. It's like "One Piece at a Time." It was really what I wanted to do. I couldn't have been happier unless it had been a song of mine.

CARR: That song was—well, not exactly socially acceptable, you know what I mean? I mean, it was really nice to hear you sticking it to the car companies.

CASH: Well, it's maybe back a bit more towards a more realistic outlook on life, y'know? There's so many people that would like to rip off the factory. It's not a sentiment that's totally far out for me, because I worked at Fisher Body Company making 1951 Pontiacs in 1950. I worked as a punch press operator in Pontiac, Michigan, in the factory—so I kinda had an understanding about what I was singing.

CARR: Would you say that the sentiments of the song echoed your own feelings, then?

CASH: Probably did so. I was eighteen years old, broke, hitchhiked to Pontiac, Michigan, got a job in the car factory and there was all this wealth of car parts rolling down the assembly line and these brand new '51 Pontiacs coming off the other end . . . I guess every one of us in that place had thoughts about driving home one of those things. Or someday owning this construction company. Y'know, everybody that's ever worked cleaning up trash for a construction company has had these thoughts at the back of his mind . . . "One of these days, I'm gonna own this construction company!" Well, I felt that way about Fisher Body Company. So when the song came along, it was like memory time for me.

CARR: There was a lot of pretty hot picking on the album— a touch of the old boogie-woogie there. Are we likely to be hearing more of that from you? It's not something you've done much of in the past.

CASH: Yeah, I think so. "City Jail," a song I just wrote for the next album, has that boogie-woogie in there. Jerry [Hensley] is on all my sessions now, so you'll be hearing more from him.

CARR: Have you been writing much lately?

CASH: Ah—I haven't written anything in about a month or so, but I write in cycles, y'know. Like, when I was getting ready to do this last album, I wrote like a house on fire. And when I get ready to work on the next album, that'll inspire me to write some more. Yeah, I have some ideas that I'll be working on.

CARR: You know, there's an awful lot of emotional range between a song like "Sold Out of Flagpoles" and one like "Committed to Parkview."

CASH: Well, they're from two different slices of life, and life is made up of all kinds of highs and lows, ups and downs—emotions. "Sold Out of Flagpoles" is the light, up side, and "Committed to Parkview" is the valley. "Committed to Parkview" was somewhere . . . I've been. I still write about things I remember. I still sing "Sunday Morning Coming Down" 'cause it's something you don't shake in seven years, that kind of life. You might have become a different person, you don't live that way anymore, but it's sure not easy to forget the bad times. For the time I was singing "Committed to Parkview" I was there.

CARR: Do you still have a bad time sometimes? Temptation? Despair?

CASH: No, I'm never in despair. I'm never depressed. I got a lot on my mind sometimes, and it might appear like I'm depressed, but I never am. Temptation, yeah. I haven't fallen to it, but it still gnaws at me. It's a daily fight. But I can't afford the luxury of taking a drink or taking a pill because I'd have to have another one if I did. I know that. 'Cause you see, even after I quit in '67, I goofed up a few times. Several times. Nobody read about it in the papers, but I did, like when I went to the Far East in '69 and when I was in California cutting the San Quentin album. There were three or four times when I had to keep relearning my lesson that I can't mess with it, or I'm dead. And I know that's where I'd be if I got back into that stuff. It's either a matter of life or death with me. I either don't do it and live, or I do it and die. That's the way it is.

CARR: Is it a hard fight?

CASH: No, it's not really, because I got it all together family-wise, love affair–wise, and everything else. I'm very much in love with my wife. I don't have any desire to fool around, and I really don't like liquor anyway. I know I'd really get a kick out of the pills for a while, but I can't do that. No, I'm really happy. I really think I'm a well-adjusted man.

CARR: You carry a lot of responsibility . . .

CASH: Uh-huh. You bet.

CARR: You're a figurehead, a target . . . does that bother you?

CASH: Being a figurehead and a target and carrying a lot of responsibility? Yeah, I get, er, I really get tired of the responsibility I have to bear. But being what I am, and with the success that's come my way, that's all a part of it. Sometimes I really get tired of it. Sometimes I really want to shake it all off and go sit under a tree all day and forget who I am and where I am. That doesn't happen very often, 'cause, you know, I enjoy being Johnny Cash, I really do. Today at that press conference, all that attention—anybody would have to be crazy not to like being admired and respected that much, to have all these people fly in from all over the country just to sit and talk to me. I enjoy being Johnny Cash most of the time.

The only thing that really irritates me—and it really irritates me badly, to where I might use a little force—is these people . . . I've seen them at my office all day long, and I've seen them on the road between my office and my house, I've waited while they got out of my way so I can drive out of my driveway, I've stopped to take the pictures and sign autographs and talk to them (and I talk to them every time). And yet, when I get ready for bed and I bed down with my family for the night, they come knocking at my door. That . . . really . . . irritates me, and I'm not gonna be responsible for what I say and do. I'm sorry to say I've really been rude to a few people. I just explode, y'know, when they coming knocking at ten o'clock and say, "I've driven a thousand miles, and you gotta talk to me." But the responsibility of living up to people's expectations about what they want me to be—being a figurehead—I don't mind that. I got a lot of self-confidence. I can handle any situation I've been faced with in that line.

CARR: What kind of a feeling do you get about the industry these days, John? You know, about how the music's going, how the controls are operating . . . the Outlaws thing, for instance?

CASH: I think all of that's good, y'know. And it's nothing new. The more change there is, the healthier the whole picture is. We can't lay back on our accomplishments and achievements . . . you know, "when this runs out I'll just quit." Now, so far as the directions in the business, the Outlaws, I think that's just another way of saying "new direction." Waylon, Willie, Tompall, all of them are saying the same things, but they're saying them differently, and as an artist, I really appreciate that. Y'know, myself, back in '56, I had a hard time breaking into the country music community in Nashville. I came up to the Grand Ole Opry to talk to Jim Denny, who was the manager of the Opry. "I Walk the Line" was Number One. I had an appointment—finally, my manager had gotten me an appointment—but I sat in his outer office about two hours before he ever saw me. Finally, he let me come in, and the very first question was "What makes you think you belong on the Grand Ole Opry?" See, I was one of those Memphis rockabillies—had sideburns—from that Memphis school of Presley, and Perkins, and Lewis, and Orbison, and Cash. It was a wonder they even let us in the city limits, the way they looked down at us at the time. Elvis had had a bad experience there—a very disappointing, unsettling experience.

But Jim Denny asked me that question. I believe I'd just read Dale Carnegie's *How to Win Friends and Influence People* or some such thing, so I sat back and collected my thoughts after such a brusque, abrupt invitation to conversation, and I said, "Well, I love country music—always sung it—and besides that, I have a Number One country record." He sat and looked at me for five minutes before he ever answered me, and then he said, "When do you think you can come up here?" But that first night, I got the feeling backstage at the Opry that there were a few of them weren't too happy to have me there. A few of them were maybe afraid of the competition (something I've really learned to appreciate is competition), but there were some of them like June Carter who really made me feel welcome. She'd worked shows with Elvis, you know, knew the Memphis scene. Then there was Minnie Pearl, and Roy Acuff, Hank Snow. Y'see, guys like Acuff and Hank Snow are smart enough to know that people's tastes change. How many decades had they been singing, even in 1956? Acuff's smart enough to know that new people are gonna come along and be accepted, but that doesn't necessarily mean the old ones have to go cut their throats. Hank Snow had befriended Elvis. There were a few small minds who wouldn't talk to us as we walked by, but I made it. It took a while, though. But back to your question. Rebels are going to come along and if they're not accepted they're gonna rebel until somebody notices them. But the thing that has been noticed about some of these rebels like Waylon is the talent. Who's going to deny Waylon's talent?

CARR: You have any gripes about the industry?

CASH: Well, the record companies in our business are all looking for the "crossover" record, and the Nashville hype is the big thing going around. These radio stations all over the country get a call from a promoter or publicist or public relations person in Nashville, saying, "Jump on this one, it's a crossover record." The whole deal is trying to cut a country song with a crossover sound, a crossover feel, so it'll get on the pop stations. My friend Hugh Cherry talks about us standing in danger of country music losing its identity or its net worth, maybe, by concentrating on crossover and not concentrating on good country, and I think there's a lot in what he has to say. I'm proud of the fact that my big crossover songs—"I Walk the Line" or "Folsom Prison Blues" were country. In no way were they an attempt to cut a crossover song. They made it over into the other markets on their own merits. The whole big thing now is to cut a record that'll blanket all the stations across the board, right off, and I think the music, the songs, the records are suffering. A lot of songs that could have been good country records aren't anything, because such an attempt was made to make them crossovers. You know, take Waylon. I can't remember hearing a record Waylon cut that sounded anything like an obvious attempt to put out a crossover record. Every record I've heard of Waylon has just been Waylon.

CARR: John, who would you pick for the CMA Awards this year?

CASH: Male Vocalist, Waylon. Female Vocalist? Looks like Tanya Tucker. Country Music Hall of Fame—Merle Travis.

Merle Travis or Kitty Wells. They both deserve it, even though I'm one of the finalists. I was really surprised when I saw I was on the list . . . really felt twenty years older.

CARR: John, what do you think of Jimmy Carter?

CASH: I knew you were gonna get around to this. How many political questions you got here, Patrick? Looks like a bunch.

CARR: C'mon, John, you worry too much. That's my shopping list. There's only one question. Really, now—what do you think of him?

CASH: Well, I think Jimmy Carter is part of the whole air of positivity in politics that has come around recently in healing this country's experience from Watergate and Vietnam. Now, Jimmy Carter—some of those who say they're voting for him are doing it because they believe what he believes, and some of them are voting for him because he believes in something. Whatever they do or not, they're voting for him because he believes in something. "I'm not sure I do, but I know he does, so I'll vote for him . . ." That's the feeling I get from some people. I think he'll probably be the next president, and I think everything's gonna be all right. On the other side . . . well, you didn't ask me that, so I ain't gonna tell you.

CARR: Mr. Ford?

CASH: Looks like he's done a pretty good job.

JUNE CARTER: I like Jimmy Carter best 'cause of family ties.

CASH: Jimmy Carter's June's fourth cousin, I believe it is. Yeah, they're cousins. He brought it up. He's the one who told her where the family ties lie. She was really surprised. He'd told her that before, kidding, y'know, but recently he told her the names—how they're related.

But I really think he will be the next president, and I guess that would be all right.

CARR: You feel OK about that, huh?

CASH: Yeah, I think I'm going to vote for him. I think I am. I'm not going to say for sure, but I told him I was gonna vote for him. That was about three months ago, and I haven't changed my mind yet.

CARR: Has he asked you to work for him?

CASH: Yes, he did. I haven't replied to that request except . . . well, I don't think it would be fair for me to campaign for a presidential candidate and try to influence people that way. That's important stuff and big stuff, and I don't think I've got a right to exercise any such control over the people. Voting is kind of a sacred, precious thing in this country . . . You're the first person in the press I've ever told about voting for Carter. I'm not recommending that anyone else vote for him; I just think I'm going to. I didn't refuse to work for Jimmy. Jimmy just mentioned that he'd like for me to make an appearance with him later on this year in a key place, but I'm not sure I'm gonna be able to do that.

CARR: Along with Jimmy Carter comes the whole notion that the South is going to be in the driver's seat if he gets elected. I wonder if you think that there's something about the South—some basic virtues, whatever—that might not go amiss in Washington? You know—the politics of love, the stress of family ties, all that?

CASH: Yeah, but you know, I think that's a false impression that those kind of things like solid family ties are characteristically southern. Or that faith in God is characteristically southern. I think that's a misconception, an untrue philosophy about the South. I think that if it holds true there, it holds true in Michigan. I think that probably there may be a spirit of strength that's stronger in the South, in what people very loosely refer to as the Bible Belt. I think that anybody with that spiritual strength would be a better president, a better leader, that that kind of mood and atmosphere and reliance upon . . . I think a man like that would do a better job. I'd feel safer with him in there, y'know . . . a man who relied upon that spiritual power to determine his decisions, that spiritual discretion, 'cause it gives him a sense of conscience, like a compass. And that really works—I know that for a fact, from personal experience. That conscience is awfully important, I think, when you're dealing with the lives of millions of people. Again, I don't know if the South's got anything over any other part of the country along that line. They show more dirty movies in the South than they do anywhere else . . . I just don't know. All this doesn't answer your question very well, but I don't know how to.

CARR: I think it does, y'know. You did raise the question of moral integrity—spiritual integrity—and that's not insignificant

CASH: "Integrity" I guess, is the word I'm trying to say. I feel that Jimmy Carter has that integrity. Not that Ford doesn't—he has that compass, too—but we're choosing a new man, and Jimmy's my choice of the new ones that are on the horizon and trying for the job.

"JOHNNY CASH'S FREEDOM" (1978)

PATRICK CARR: The last time we talked, John, you spoke about making albums more like the old Johnny Cash . . . You know, without a lot of fancy orchestration and stuff.

JOHNNY CASH: Yes, well, that's what we're trying to do. We're trying to make it sound a bit more like something that was done today, rather than back in 1955, but we had a lot of things going on the *Gone Girl* album. First of all we had fun making it, we enjoyed it. We had my people that I enjoy working with—the Carter Family, Jan Howard, my group—and Jack Clement came in and played rhythm guitar. He's always a ball on sessions—or, usually, anyway. Yes we enjoyed doing the album.

Larry Butler had been busy producing some big hit art-ist, and about the time that I wanted to do the album he was right in the middle of it. I had to wait a while, and I got a little frustrated, and he knew I got a little frustrated, and finally we got together on a date. We didn't have words of anything, but I wanted in the studio. You know—when I wanted in, I wanted *in*.

The album came after a trip that June and Jan Howard and Jack Clement and I took to New York City. We went up and saw a couple of plays, and we sat up at night and picked and sang, and we got into some old songs like "A Bar with No Beer" and "Careless Love" and "Always Alone" and "Born to Love," all those old things. Then we got into bluegrass, up-tempo stuff. Then we got to doing Jagger and Richard's song "No Expectations," and Jack said, "Let's do it bluegrass style." I said, "It don't quite fit bluegrass style, but let's do it up-tempo," so we got to doing "No Expectations." Jan Howard knew it—she'd sung it before on the Grand Ole Opry—so she gave us the words for it. So we sang "No Expectations" perhaps forty times during the whole evening, and when we quit singing it the people next door called the room and said, "Please play some more!" We thought we'd been keeping ev-erybody up.

That's the kind of spirit we had in the studio when we recorded the album—you know, we were having fun.

The musicians know that, too, see. It's awfully impor-tant to the musicians to feel that the artist is not acting like a star and not acting like the boss; he's acting like somebody that you're having fun with. That's what my guys felt in that studio that day. They were talking and laughing and cutting up and kidding Jack Clement about this and that, trying to make him balance a glass on the top of his head and do different kinds of dances. So we just had a lot of fun. Everybody was loose and laughing, and that's what helped to make it work.

But way before that I did a lot of homework. I weeded out a whole lot of songs. There were a lot of songs I didn't record on that album that I *wanted* to record, because I've been looking for good songs. You know who I've been listening to a lot? Tom T. Hall. Tom T. Hall has got to be the greatest country songwriter alive. I went to the K-Mart to buy a Tom T. Hall album the other day, just to hear some more of his songs. So I've got some of his songs laid back that I want to do—things he did on albums and didn't release as singles. But he's got so much great stuff.

It's not only him, either. There's other people like Rodney Crowell. Rodney has some good songs, and I'm holding some of his. I wanted to do some more of his on the album, but I didn't have room for them. So I'm looking forward to my next album, and I'm going to do my homework before I go in. And if everybody's not enjoying themselves and having fun when we get in the studio, then we'll just go home.

CARR: Cancel the session?

CASH: Right. After all these years, I realize that it's not especially the quality of the studio, who's got the best equipment, who's got the best sound. Jack Clement Studio happens to have a *great* sound and *great* equipment, which is why I picked that studio at that time, but I may do another session at the Quonset Hut, Columbia Studio B, where I recorded so many times. I think I may do my next album there, because it'd be like memory time for me. Back in the sixties I was there so many times with the Statler Brothers and the Carter Family and my group, back in times when I was having my own particular kind of fun and everyone else was sitting around waiting for old Johnny Cash to get ready to record—but now I think we could go back in there and have a good time. We may go back there, or we may go back to Jack Clement's studio, but either way . . .

CARR: The key to it all is atmosphere, right?

CASH: Exactly. Well, first of all, there's the songs. So I'm going to do my homework. Do a lot of listening to Tom T. Hall and Rodney Crowell and some other people.

CARR: What other people?

CASH: Well, I really like John Prine and Steve Goodman. I got two of their songs I'm going to try, see if the feeling's right. I've got several songs myself. I've been writing like crazy. I've got enough for an album of my own things that I've written since we did the *Gone Girl* album.

CARR: Things sound good. Sounds like you're really cooking these days . . .

CASH: Well, you know I've sold my recording studio 'cause I never was interested in it in the first place. I don't know why

I ever wanted one out here. I guess I do, too: because I could get Charlie Bragg to run it, and I believed in him as an engineer. But now we've gotten rid of that studio, which became kind of a burden, and Charlie's got a good job somewhere else, and the girls downstairs are turning it into a museum—which leaves me free. I guess that's it. That's another word that is important in this, too, Patrick. I feel free, you know. If I want to go to California and record, I'll do it. I'm not saying I will, but I might.

CARR: It's getting some of that big Cash load off your back, all those responsibilities . . .

CASH: That's right. They're usually the ones I want to bear anyway, but things like that studio you look back on and say, "Hey, that was a status symbol, an ego trip. What'd I do that for? That was stupid. I don't do that no more." But I'm free, you see. I'm free to go where I want to and record with whoever I want to.

CARR: That seems to be the direction you've been heading in for the last three years or so.

CASH: Yes. Freedom is the word. Not only that kind of freedom we were talking about, but freeing yourself from ideas and preconceived notions about what is expected of you. I forgot all of that crap. Forget about that I don't think about what is expected of me anymore. I'm doing what I *feel* is right for me.

For instance, I have people who say to me, "I want you

to sound like you did in 1955 on Sun." I can't sing that way anymore, and people don't record that way anymore. Well, there's one cut on the *Gone Girl* album, "I Will Rock and Roll with You," where I asked them to put that old Sun slap-back on, and it's pretty much got that old Sun sound. So we'll give them a little bit of that if they ask for it, if people want to hear it. I mean, I can do that electronically. But honesty in performance and freedom of delivery, that's where it's at. I feel free in the studio now. I wish I could go back in and do the *Gone Girl* album over again, and if I did, do you know what I'd do? I'd do it *exactly* the way I did.

CARR: Has Jack Clement had much to do with this kind of spirit in you?

CASH: Well, I haven't seen him in about two months, but I'm going to call him and pick his brains and see what kind of songs he's got. Jack has got so many great songs that he's forgotten about, you know, and I have to sit down with him and swap songs. "Hey, here's one I wrote that I forgot about!" he'll say, and he'll sing this song that you know should have been a hit when he wrote it. So I'm going to sit down with Jack and see if he's got anything else I might record, and then I'm probably going to ask him to come play rhythm with me again, 'cause I like to work with him. As a matter of fact, Jack Clement asked me to produce his next album.

CARR: Really? That's a switch, isn't it?

CASH: Yeah, that scared me so bad. I haven't even answered him yet. I said, "What do you mean, produce you?" He said, "Oh, come down and sit in and play rhythm with me and tell me when I'm doing something wrong." I said, "Man, you sure are giving me too much credit here. I'm not a producer. I don't want to be a producer." He said, "Well, just come on down, sit in with me and play rhythm with me." I said, "All right, I'll do that."

CARR: John, how did all this freedom business start? I mean, you really weren't like this a few years ago.

CASH: You know what? It's just going back to the basics of what it was like back before all the big years of success and all that stuff. It was freedom, and I'm just looking for that freedom again. I've seen that in people like Waylon. Waylon is more free inside, and free from the business world of the music business, than anybody I know. He demands his privacy, demands exclusiveness to be not involved in everything going around. I guess maybe that my late association with people like Waylon—like, I learned a lot from Waylon. I mean, I can handle people. I like people, and I can handle them by the dozen—you know, when they come to the shows, I can handle them backstage and all that—but Waylon handles them with so much patience because he knows that tomorrow, ain't nobody in the *world* gonna be able to find him because he's going to be hiding out resting somewhere. Tomorrow, everybody in the world will know where Johnny Cash is, 'cause I'll have a commitment somewhere. That's the way it's been, but I've become a little bit harder to get to. Maybe I'm going through the change of life or something, but I want more time for myself, and I want more freedom from worry and work and the hassle that goes on at the offices and the recording studios.

CARR: It's showing in the music, you know.

CASH: Well, I hope it'll show more the next time around. Like I said, if the feeling's not there, we won't record. We won't do it until the feeling *is* there.

CARR: What about working with Waylon? Are you still getting him into the studio with you?

CASH: Well, he and I have done two more songs, but the record companies are having a hassle over who's going to release it. We just did a duet that RCA Victor gave CBS permission to release, but I don't know about Waylon's status with his record company, so I don't know if that song's going to be released or not. So we got two things we're holding, and we don't have any plans to record anything more right now. We have talked about sometime doing an album if we can get enough songs that feel right, but we don't have enough songs yet. I don't talk to Waylon very often, really, 'cause he travels like I do.

CARR: What do you think about what Carl Perkins is doing these days, John?

CASH: I think it's great. He's really hot again in England. Ol' *Blue Suede Shoes* is back, that's a great album. Carl Perkins is better than he's ever been. He was always great, but now he's better than he's ever been, 'cause he's free too, you know? For a long time he was the opener for the Johnny Cash Show, and I never did feel right about it. I never did feel right about having an artist of his stature in that position. But that's what he wanted, and it worked for a long time. When he went off on his own is when he really came *into* his own, though. He's terrific. He's got it all together, in his head and his heart.

CARR: He's sort of like you seem to be right now—he's got his family and his music, and he's doing what he wants to do. He's free to play.

CASH: Yes, sir. He's the best there is, in his field.

CARR: You think things are loosening up in the country music business in general, John? Last time I asked you that, about two years ago, you said basically that maybe they were, but you weren't too sure.

CASH: I don't know. I don't read the trades. I look at the charts every week if *Cashbox* or *Billboard* or *Record World* happens to be on my desk, but I don't really know what direction country music is going in. I'm really concerned with which direction *I'm* going in.

CARR: Maybe you're pulling back from your role as figurehead of the country music business?

CASH: I didn't know that's what I was. I don't know what that means, really.

CARR: Yes. No good asking you that these days, is it?

CASH: They keep asking me every year to host the annual CMA Awards show, and I kind of hope they don't ask me anymore. I get a little embarrassed. Really, I keep thinking some of my peers are going to say, "Hey, what? We got to have him again?" But the network keeps asking for me. I enjoy doing it, but I know there's that other world of country music out there that is as important to the people as that CMA world. It's a weird thing for someone like me to say, but I know that there's two worlds of country music out there now. There's that CMA world and there's that other world.

CARR: What's the other world?

CASH: Well, there's Waylon and Willie and all the guys that you don't see on the CMA—great artists like Marty Robbins, Webb Pierce, Carl Smith, Ferlin Husky, Faron Young, Ernest Tubb, Hank Snow. All these are great, great country artists, and you don't see them on the CMA show. You don't see them as a guest or a presenter, even. The network is looking for names, for ratings, and they don't realize how important some of these names really are. But there's no greater country singer than Marty Robbins, and I've asked the last two years to get Marty Robbins on the show, and I get some kind of runaround. And I'm not really all that happy to be the host of the show for that reason. Tom T. Hall—have you ever seen Tom T. Hall on that show? That's what bugs me. That's what really gets to me, that the agent and I will talk it over, and he'll say, "Well, what do you recommend I do?" and he'll say,

"Well, you're the only one that means anything to them rat-ings-wise." I say, "Well, I don't *believe* that." Then we'll talk about the people that are going to be on it. I'll say, "Are they going to have any of the people on it that they've neglected in the past?" He'll say, "I don't have anything to do with that." Then I'll finally get around to talking to the producer. "Oh, the talent's already set for the show." That's about as far as I get. I guess it's about time that I did let them know that I'm really galled that they don't have great people like Tom T. Hall and Marty Robbins and Ferlin Husky on there. I mean, Ferlin Husky's an entertainer. He's one of the greatest the business ever had. And just 'cause he doesn't have a hot record right now doesn't mean he's not important. There's a lot of them out there that are important.

Then there's the other world of country music like Way-lon and Willie or Charlie Daniels—oh, Charlie was on there this year—and the other guys who couldn't care less about the CMA or anything else that goes on, only with what they're doing and the way they want to do it, like I am right now. The way I feel about the *Gone Girl* album is I guess the way these guys feel about most everything in the business—"If it don't feel right, I ain't going to get in it." I get into a lot of things in the music business that don't feel right but I get involved in them because of who I am. Whatever that means.

CARR: How do you feel about Jimmy Carter these days, John?

CASH: I'm not going to talk to you about politics.

CARR: Can I press you on one point? When we last talked, you said that you hoped Jimmy Carter might just bring back a sense of honesty and Christian values to this country. Do you think that has happened, if only a little?

CASH: Well, it's happened to me personally, and it's happened to a lot of people around me. Jimmy Carter's been up and down in the polls, but I think he's been as good a president as a president can be. I can't imagine any man even being able to handle the job in the first place. Any man that can bear it and keep grinning like he does has to be quite a man. But I don't believe that he's directly responsible for any great Christian revival—no. There's been a lot written about his being born again, and it's become a joke in a lot of areas—even though it's not a joke, it's a spiritual truth—but no, no great spiritual revival has taken place in this country that I can see. As a matter of fact, I've seen more decadence in the last couple of years than I've ever seen before in my whole life, I believe.

But the churches are full. But you know what, Patrick? I read a book recently called *In His Steps*. It was written in 1896, and in this book the man talks about the Church and how it separates itself from the very ones who need it most—the poor, the needy—and this preacher challenges his congregation in this book to go out next week and do it as Jesus would do it. Whatever you do, whatever you say, you ask yourself, "Is this the way Jesus would do it?" and see what comes about. So there was a lot of people in the congregation took the challenge, and started going out among the poor people and giving them food packages. They started putting their Christianity into action. Stopped separating themselves in their beautiful white sepulcher of a church from the poor people, the hungry people in the slums and the ghettos. Like I say, the churches are full, but the slums and the ghettos are still full, and for the most part, the churches and the needy haven't quite gotten together yet. And until more people in the Church realize the real needs of the people, and go out rather than going in . . . I mean, to go into church is great, but to go out, and put it all into action, that's where it's all at. And I haven't seen a lot of action.

CARR: One of the things I've always liked about you is that you are a committed Christian, and yet still work and hang around with people who might be considered backsliders or might have supposedly non-Christian habits. Funky musicians, you know? And you seem to be able to inhabit both worlds.

CASH: Well, it's not like going both ways. I don't compromise. I don't compromise my religion. If I'm with someone who doesn't want to talk about it, I don't talk about it. I don't talk about it. I don't impose myself on anybody in *any* way, including religion. When you're imposing you're offending, I feel. Although I *am* evangelical and I'll give the message to anyone that wants to hear it, or anybody that is willing to listen. But if they let me know that they don't want to hear it, they ain't ever going to hear it from me. If I *think* they don't want to hear it, then I will not bring it up.

It's something that Waylon and I have never discussed, and we're the best of friends. We've got into some deep subjects like—well, we got into religion a little bit; not much, but we got into some deep stuff. I never got into it with Kris

Kristofferson, really. Even when I was doing *Gospel Road* and he was around, we really didn't talk about it much 'cause, you know, some people are uncomfortable talking about it. But back to how Jesus did it. He was that way, and I'm trying to be like him.

CARR: John, is there anything you'd like to say about Mother Maybelle?

CASH: Mother Maybelle Carter. I still get choked up. She was my fishing buddy. That was my relationship with her. I've just lost an old buddy. That's it, and I don't have too much to say. She was the greatest. She was the first and the greatest and the music world will slowly but surely begin playing its tributes to her by people recording everything she ever wrote and recorded.

CARR: I was talking to Carl Perkins the day after she died, and he said much the same thing. He said that when he was on the road with you, he and Mother Maybelle used to sit up at night playing cards, and that's how he'd always think of her.

CASH: I did a lot of that. We'd play poker. We'd sit up all night playing poker with Mother Maybelle.

CARR: What about Elvis, John? Any last words on Elvis?

CASH: Well, what has not been said? Elvis was the greatest in *his* field, of course. I'd always admired him. Every show before I went in, I'd always watch every minute of his show from the side. But I didn't see Elvis for the last eighteen years of his life, so I didn't know him that well.

CARR: What did the commercialization after his death do to you?

CASH: Well, I didn't go out and buy a bunch of posters and junk they were selling, but it's something I expected. I'll tell you what it's done, though—it's got him a whole new world of fans. Little kids. Every little kid loves Elvis Presley. Kids John Carter's age, eight years old. I take him to school, he's singing "All Shook Up" or "Jailhouse Rock" or something, every day. Every little kid knows Elvis.

CARR: Sounds sort of like 1953 all over again.

CASH: No, I'm talking about little bitty kids, you know?

CARR: Well, it makes a change from John Travolta, eh?

CASH: Right.

"RING OF FIRE"

INTERVIEW BY GLENN JORGENSON
RIVER PARK PRODUCTIONS
IT'S GREAT TO BE ALIVE
1983

GLENN JORGENSON: First of all, John, I want to thank you really for taking the time in a really strenuous schedule to appear with us on our *It's Great to Be Alive* series. And I am just really grateful because I know someone out there is going to get some help from the program and the comments that will go back and forth between us, so thank you very much, John.

JOHNNY CASH: It is my pleasure, and the one who is probably going to get the help is me because I have a habit of feeding off people like you who's got some real strength to offer people. For all us old down-and-outers and hard-timers, it is still one day at a time. Every day an inspiration comes along like this program, and it really means a lot.

JORGENSON: John, we really appreciate you, and I want to share with you that, when I first met you in early 1970s, I was early in my recovery. You were the right person at the right time because you gave me some early inspiration. There was an air that came from you. I really don't know how to describe it, but when I shook your hand, I could feel it. A strength, a spirituality, and an acceptance on your part. I've often wondered what makes Johnny Cash a legend, institution, inspiration to people, and with your permission, I would like to discuss some of the things that went into creating a person who has been able to help so many people . . .

As I said, I am very appreciative of you taking the time and helping us to help a whole lot of people. My first recollection of you, when I first met you in the early seventies, I was struck by something in you that came out in the form of strength, acceptance, almost like a spirituality, which was important to me, John, because at that time, I was early into my own recovery from chemical addiction. I've often wondered what creates a John Cash who can have that power and that ability to convey the message. Of course, it is in the giving away that we keep it, I know. I'd like to talk about those things. When did you first get introduced to chemicals? What was it like in those early days?

CASH: It was beautiful. People take drugs because it makes you feel good. Like I pointed out in my book, there is a demon called deception that is like the old wino. He drinks out of the bottle so long, then the bottle starts drinking out of him. Oh, the pills. I took the pills so long, and the reversal came without me knowing it, when the pills started taking from me. I had seven years of constant habituation and addiction. It was cold hard addiction, devotion. I mean it was devotion to what I was doing. It was amphetamines, barbiturates, and alcohol, all three in a cycle for seven years. I am six-foot-two, and when I, through God, found the strength to come out of it in 1967, I weighed one hundred and fifty-two pounds, which is fifty pounds less than what I weigh now.

I knew you felt the spirit there. I am really glad to hear that because it was a spirit of the love of God that made a survivor out of me. It is the love and care from people like yourself and my wife June Carter, who every day I feel the touch of caring that has made not only a survivor but a sustainer. It is not an easy road to go on. It is a very lonely fight. It is good to turn from your lonely struggle and find somebody behind you who cares and helps you out. Ready to inspire you, ready to give you strength and encouragement. People on drugs, habituated to a chemical, if, when they decide to kick it, and only they can decide, no one can decide for them. When they decide to stop it, if they have somebody who really loves them whom they can cling to, you got to shake off the old man. As Paul says, you have to throw off the old life and put on the new. I found myself having to close the door on some old friends because they wanted to keep me down where they were. Regardless of what people call me or thought of me, I knew I needed, that God wanted me to live, so I clung to the people who I knew cared and had his love in their lives.

JORGENSON: I think we who make it back, God saw some good in us that could help other people. We, who did, tried everything there was to overcome this dependency and addiction. It was only when I gave up that I began to win. From reading your book and knowing this part of your life, was there a point where you surrendered and gave up?

CASH: There was.

JORGENSON: What was the key time, key elements, key cursor? What was involved in the miracle in your life in which you finally said I give up?

CASH: Well I roughly described my condition in '67 when I came out of the addiction, but if you had a picture of me at that time, you wouldn't believe it was me. I was a spelunker. There is a cave near Chattanooga, Tennessee, that I like to explore. There is a big room in there where Civil War soldiers stayed, and no one really knows where all of the caverns go. I've been in there several times with my friends. Every time I would get high, I would get in my jeep or truck and head for Chattanooga to the people who, I thought, would put up with me—you know? I knew I had worn out my welcome with everyone in Nashville from keeping them up all night and this and that.

But, finally, even my friends in Chattanooga couldn't really put up with me any longer. I saw it. I had turned my back on June and on my own mother, and she had given up on me and driven back to California where she lived and had a slight heart attack on the way. At that time, that didn't bother me in the least because there is one thing about someone addicted to pills and alcohol. They're very selfish, you know? They don't care about anybody but themselves and the way they happen to feel right now. That's all I cared about, all I talked about. How I feel, what I want for me, you know? I disregarded my four daughters in California and my mother.

But June Carter was a fighter. And I couldn't get over what I had done to my mother . . . June found out where I was and came to my friend's house in Chattanooga, looking for me. I found out she was coming, so I went to the cave twenty miles away. I had been up two or three days and nights when she got there, so I took my beer that I was drinking—I was drinking a case of beer a day and taking up to a hundred pills, half amphetamines and half barbiturates, to keep me going up and down and keep the cycle going. I was sweating the beer out—so the only calories I guess were from hops and malt.

I remember sitting in the mouth of that cave crying and taking a little two-cell flashlight and walking into that cave. I decided that I would walk as far as I could go and lay down. I guess I probably went about a mile through one of the caverns, and my flashlight completely burned out. It was black, so dark that you could feel it. I lay down flat on my back and said my goodbye prayers. *I can't handle it myself. I am giving up. I am going.* I must have dozed off because I felt a presence. I didn't see anything; I didn't hear anything, but I felt a presence. I felt a power and a strength, and that inner voice almost said, "No, you don't give up. You got things to do." I mean, I am not saying that God talked to me, but I felt that power within me come from outside of me to make me sit up and look around. I couldn't see any light. But . . . this is awfully corny, but the old Indian trick is to lick your finger and stick it up and see which way the wind blows. I tried everything to see, and then I finally did that and felt cool air on one side of my finger and knew. I kept following it and crawling. Sometimes, I would fall thirty feet into a pit, but I would crawl my way back up. Just as I was about to give up, I saw a little fleck of light off in the distance. I started crawling and clawing toward that entrance. I finally made it there, and I collapsed in the mouth of the cave. I told a little about that in this book, but I didn't go into the detail that I am going now. In the mouth of this cave, when I awoke, June was there with my friends from Chattanooga. She knew it was really, really bad this time.

I had a psychiatrist friend, the commissioner of mental

health for Tennessee, who is also a country musician. I woke up, and June was washing my face, and she said, "You're almost dead, aren't you?" I said, "You're calling that Winston. I want to live." She said, "Are you sure?" I said, "Yep, I want to go with you." So she took me back to Nashville, and we called our friend. He came out and looked at me, and he said later, "I wouldn't have given you a 1/1000 chance for making it." He said, "You were so hooked and wrapped up in your own self and your own addiction." Winston questioned me, "Are you deadly serious? Have you personally decided that you're going to quit?" I said, "Yes, sir." He said, "I'll be here every day, thirty minutes after I get off work." And he was, for thirty days. He was there every day at 5:30 p.m. Knowing that Winston was coming back, and June, her mother and daddy, and all my family and friends were downstairs sleeping in sleeping bags in this big house that I had bought on the lake—it kept me going. They started, a week into breaking this addiction, bringing me food. The nightmares continued for about three weeks without letup every time I closed my eyes. The hardest thing to break was the downers. Dr. Winston told me I would crave amphetamines or want them every day for the rest of my life, and I guess he's right because it's a one day at a time battle. Back then, I was taking equinel, meprobamate, ethinamate. I burned my stomach out from my beer, and I think the popular thing today is Valium. I think that's the little demon called deception today.

JORGENSON: Valium and Librium.

CASH: Librium, too. I almost got wrapped up in the whole cycle again because a doctor prescribed Librium for something for me that he thought I needed it for, and I didn't realize what it was. It's one of those tricky little things that feels good and grabs hold of you.

JORGENSON: Well, one of the sad parts is people are still, and we're getting better, but they have not come to understand that those so-called mild tranquilizers are very addicting. Part of the purpose of the work we're doing is trying to get them aware that these are not to be used for a way of life. There may be certain conditions that would be proper to use them, but to make them an ongoing thing, such as you and I did, that's hell. You start out thinking you've found the keys to heaven, but you found the keys to hell.

CASH: Those pills should be named Delilah. They're sweet to touch and look at. It's good to try them, to window shop, but if you stay with them for too long, you get your head cut off. Not just your hair, but your head.

JORGENSON: And I wish there was, too . . . So that is more or less when you decided to quit cold turkey.

CASH: I didn't have any medication to taper off on. It was cold turkey, but like I said, love and care of June, my mother, our families, and Dr. Winston.

JORGENSON: I know from my profession that what you experienced and what you survived is a miracle. I know that that combination, that heavy and that long, could have been totally disastrous.

CASH: I know.

JORGENSON: John, in the limits of time that we have, what's life like now as opposed to that?

CASH: Well, it's still a struggle because the lifestyle I live is unbelievable to people. They say, "What have you been doing lately?" And I say, "How lately?" Two weeks ago, I was in Budapest, Hungary. Two weeks from now, I will be in Canada, in Saskatchewan, here and there, or New York.

Sometimes we eat and sleep, and sometimes we don't. There is not a day that goes by that I don't want a mood elevator or a leveller or a sleeping pill or an upper, because of the erratic lifestyle I live. I expected to have it tougher than everybody else though. Because, in 1969–70, I had some fabulous success record-wise and television-wise. That's when I started really studying the bible in earnest, and I realized— and I won't quote it but paraphrase it—he whom much is given much is required. I realized that many times what the regular requirement was for the average person was going to be required of me to survive. I made up my mind with God's help and the love of those who care about me that I can make it. I will fight at it. I will whip it.

JORGENSON: Part of that is doing what you're doing here. The sharing and giving away adds to the strength. It is hard for people to understand that paradox, but we know that's how we are sustained. But I am sure that the realization that you are making the world a better place and you are helping people has to give you some moments of "it's great to be alive" feeling. Or feeling up.

CASH: Yes, it does.

JORGENSON: John, if you were to change anything in the world today, what would you like to change?

CASH: Well, life is so precious that I think that the grade school children should be the ones to decide on the nuclear arms balance. For one thing, if we left it up to the kids, there wouldn't be one on Earth. I think it's insanity that humankind exists with one nuclear warhead in the world.

If I could do one thing to make this world a better place, I would, there would not be one nuclear warhead anywhere in the world. If politicians could take that and work it out and get rid of them all . . . but I would also snap out the inner holocaust that so many people are into now. What I hate, what it kills me to see now, is not just the young people and the things that drugs are doing to them but what alcohol is doing to people our age. We can talk about the kids and drugs all that we want to, but I really think that the biggest drug problem we have in this country is alcoholism.

JORGENSON: No question about it, John. No question. Seven times the problem.

CASH: It is socially accepted. But in Tennessee, they have passed a law that you go to jail if you are picked up and have had two drinks in the last hour. If that was a national law, I believe people would take notice as to *Why? What is this all about?* Because it kills people. That's why.

JORGENSON: People forget that, and of course, that is a whole area of why this is a death-dealing affliction. It is insane that we aren't doing more. I often say that the drug problem is not in the streets but our medicine cabinets. We sit around discussing it with our kids with a highball in our hands. There has to be a change from the inside.

In the people I have visited, something has to occur within. You said in the beginning that it makes you feel good, so the reason we become addicted is comfort. We are uncomfortable with some aspect of our life, and we find that drugs or alcohol makes us feel better. I guess it makes sense, doesn't it? To change that to make us feel better about ourselves inside? Maybe that's where the change has to come.

CASH: A drug addict or an alcoholic will argue with you, as you know, all day long that he hasn't had a fourth as much as he really had. It is back to the old demon called deception. There are so many things in this world that can cause an inner holocaust and that can deceive us. The medication was made for a special reason, and the doctors say that they don't prescribe that because people abuse it. I don't know what people *don't* abuse. In the way of medication, I think we need more education on what the side effects to a lot of the medications are that are going around. Personally, I have the physician's desk reference in my house in three or four different rooms.

JORGENSON: You can see the indications and contraindications.

CASH: My mother and father are elderly and have to take a lot of medications; I bought it for their benefit. I've learned a lot from it.

JORGENSON: John, you've been involved in helping programs like ours in continuing to carry the message that there is hope and there is help. That's what I hear. And I hear it in your music. Is that a proper reflection on the message that you're carrying in much of your music? The hope filled?

CASH: I just finished a gospel song album, and every one of these is positive, up songs. There is a positive force, a positive power in gospel music, as there is in the Gospel. There is hope, and there is help. I don't know anyone in this world who doesn't have someone who loves them. If they can turn to that one person in times of trouble, the one person they know won't fail them . . .

JORGENSON: What would you like to be remembered for or by?

CASH: As a good daddy and husband.

JORGENSON: That's great. That's where it begins, isn't it? John Cash, it is a great pleasure. I feel honored and appreciative of you and what you're doing and your music and your entertaining and your brotherhood.

CASH: Thank you. God bless you.

JOHNNY CASH: A LAW UNTO HIMSELF

INTERVIEW BY BARNEY HOSKINS

MOJO

1996

We're passing through Andover, Kansas, scene of one of the worst tornadoes in American history: a monstrous twister that levelled the little town and took thirty lives just a few years ago. Every building in sight looks like it was put up in the last ten minutes. Human history has been eradicated here.

Early evening sunlight is streaming through the windows of the black and silver MCI Greyhound bus, bathing the monumental features of Johnny Cash in its warm orange rays. The left side of Cash's face is painfully swollen after the countless operations he's had on his jaw, but once again he is preparing himself to perform for a gathering of the country faithful, this time in what turns out to be the absolute middle of nowhere—a spanking-new shopping mall standing surreally alone in the endless flat expanse of America's Great Plains. You couldn't get much closer to the heart of Heartland USA if you tried.

Appropriately enough, since we have just left the outskirts of Wichita, Cash begins humming, and then singing, the famous Jimmy Webb song about the county lineman—"still on the line" like the equally famous protagonist of Cash's own "I Walk the Line." From the back of the bus emerges June Carter Cash, the epitome of homely southern graciousness with her hair up in a towel. She too is preparing for the umpteenth show in which she will duet with her husband on "Jackson" and "If I Were a Carpenter" and then interleave a magical medley of Carter Family classics with her hilarious comic monologues.

Sitting across from Cash at a table that folds away to become a bed, I ask him whether he is likely to sing any of the songs from his superb new album, *Unchained*, tonight. My assumption is that he'll save his versions of Beck's "Rowboat" and Soundgarden's "Rusty Cage" for the *haute*-hip scenesters of London and Manhattan and stick to staples like "Ring of Fire" and "Sunday Morning Coming Down."

"If there's a lotta young people, I'll do 'Rusty Cage,'" he says in the great deep voice, a sonorous blend of John Wayne in *The Shootist* and Robert Mitchum in *The Night of the Hunter*. "I've got to get on and feel the audience. I know how I'm gonna start off, but that's about it. College-town audiences are my favorite—that's when it feels like the fifties again. Then we go wild."

Soon the mall emerges on the level horizon; in the fading light we begin to make out the cars and pickups parked in the surrounding fields. As the bus pulls off the highway, there are scores of people waiting to watch Cash step out of the vehicle—a mass of caps and Stetsons and mullets. Cash draws the curtains to hide himself, but June waves on the other side to a middle-aged couple sitting in a Winnebago. "Our own groupies," she informs me. "They follow us everywhere."

It transpires that over 10,000 people have schlepped out on this balmy, breezy Columbus Day evening to see the show. The stage sits in the middle of the mall, a miniature golf course to one side and stores with neon-lit names like London Fog, Jones New York and Rue 21 to the other. At about eight o'clock, local KFDI jock Johnny Western takes the stage and breaks into a warm-up medley of cowboy songs. Western was Cash's support act and general road buddy during the hell-raising, pill-shovelling days of the early-to-mid-sixties, so this is something of a reunion. Between ballads, Western makes it his business to thank a large number of local dignitaries for making this event possible: the mayor, the police chief, the fire chief—and the mall's owners, natch. Seated on a stool at the side of the stage all the while is Cash himself, coughing and signing autographs for on-duty policemen.

At 8:15, Johnny Western does what he did for seven-odd years and gives his old boss the showbiz buildup: "Here he is! The Man in Black! 'I Walk the Line'! 'Ring of Fire'! 'Folsom Prison Blues'! Put your hands together for . . . Johnny Cash!!!" And slowly Cash walks on to the familiar sight of thousands of hard-working, God-fearing middle Americans risen to their feet in mass homage. People swarm to the front with their cameras, crouching below Cash to capture his majesty on a home snap.

"It's windy tonight," Cash's voice booms out of the PA. "But it's a good wind, a *Kansas* wind. You can breathe it."

He starts with "Folsom Prison Blues" and then slides into the vintage rockabilly shuffle of "Get Rhythm," a song he wrote 40 years ago for his Sun labelmate Elvis Presley. A sombre treatment of Kris Kristofferson's "Sunday Morning Coming Down" seems to connect with everyone, even if it does feature the word "stoned."

"There's some country songs on my new album that I really hope you'll get to hear," he announces, a veiled reference to the fact that 1994's Rick Rubin-produced *American Recordings* was comprehensively ignored by country radio. He sings the exquisite title track from the new album, and does it without a hint of sappiness. He tears up "Country Boy," one of two old Sun rockers reprised for *Unchained*. And then, despite the pronounced absence of anything even resembling a teenager in this crowd, he introduces "Rusty Cage."

"It's a Soundgarden song," he states, to deafening silence.

Cash's performance of Chris Cornell's song, both live and on the album, is a masterpiece of mythopoeic menace. "I'm gonna break/I'm gonna break my/I'm gonna break my rusty cage and run," he all but roars at the mall audience as the song hits its grungy climax. I stare out across the rows of farming families and wonder what they make of it. I see only blank incomprehension, and then huge relief as the band segues seamlessly into "Ring of Fire," its mariachi brass motif duplicated on a small synthesizer by pianist Earl Ball. A lady with a big Bob Dole badge rushes forward and waves her original copy of the *Ring of Fire* album at Cash. The Man in Black doesn't notice.

The fact that he went ahead and did "Rusty Cage" anyway says something about Johnny Cash. Not a lot, but something. It says that he doesn't really care whether this corn-shucking crowd objects to Soundgarden or not, just like he didn't care too much what God-fearing middle Americans in the sixties thought of his stand on issues like Vietnam, prison reform or the plight of American Indians. It says that he's not in the play-safe nostalgia business, that he needs to move forward as much as he needs to oblige diehard fans with songs he's been singing for 40 years. And it says, like almost everything he's done, that he is a law unto himself.

Right now, Johnny Cash is partway into the third wind

of his career, a new lease of life after the doldrum years of the eighties. And some wind it is turning out to be. His fellow Highwaymen (Willie Nelson, Waylon Jennings, and Kris Kristofferson) may have recorded albums with Don Was, but Cash's knight in shining armour turned out to be a long-haired New Yorker best known for loosing Public Enemy and The Beastie Boys on the world. Just as Bob Dylan had cronied with Cash in the sixties—prompting a Columbia press statement that the Man in Black had "finally been discovered by the underground"—so Cash's first album for Rick Rubin's American label has led to every two-bit grungester and super-model wanting to bask in his formidable presence. The man has become a trans-generational icon, a godfather of American Gothic, a tabula rasa for people who prefer mythology to reality. All we need now is for Johnny Depp and Kate Moss to have a baby and ask Cash to be its godfather.

For *Unchained*, the follow-up to *American Recordings*, Cash has opted for a full-band sound (essentially Tom Petty and the Heartbreakers, with assorted guests) that almost recalls the raw twang of his Sun days. It's a more accessible album than its predecessor, which wasn't so much unplugged as unclothed. It also manages to span 50 years of music—from Jimmie Rodgers's "The One Rose" to Beck's "Rowboat" via Dean Martin's "Memories Are Made of This"—without anything sounding out of place. It is, in short, one of the year's best records.

"*American Recordings* was harder," Cash tells me in his Wichita hotel room. "There was nothing to hide behind, and that was scary. With this album I had more fun because I was with a bunch of people makin' music together. It's a more musical record. The sessions felt a lot like the Memphis days . . . that kind of freedom. Sitting around and talking: 'Whaddya wanna do now?' No clock on the wall, no pressure. I'd been doing 'Country Boy' in concert, so we got into that and boy, it felt good. 'Mean-Eyed Cat' was originally written 40 years ago but never finished, so I wrote another verse about a year ago."

BARNEY HOSKYNS: I gather you were initially reluctant to cover the Beck and Soundgarden songs.

JOHNNY CASH: Well, if a song doesn't feel right, then it isn't communicating. That was the problem I had with "Rusty Cage." But Rick and Tom came up with an arrangement that was real comfortable for me, and I think it may be one of my favourite songs to perform now. "Rowboat" was another one I turned down: as it was, it wasn't for me. I couldn't see a way that I could do it.

HOSKYNS: What did you make of Beck when he opened for you in L.A. last year?

CASH: My impression was that in a way he was a great hill-billy singer. He had that Appalachian music like he really felt it and loved it.

HOSKYNS: Would you say your success with the alternative rock crowd has cost you any country fans?

CASH: No, I have not turned my back on Nashville. I don't know if they turned their back on me. Doesn't really matter, I wasn't doing anything there anyway but going through the motions. I got totally down and out with Nashville when I realised that Mercury only pressed 500 copies of the last album I did there. So why spin my wheels?

HOSKYNS: Last year you quit Branson, Missouri [country theme town where Nashville veterans perform for package tourists] when you were only getting 300 people in a 3,000-capacity theatre. I wondered if the heartland country fans had abandoned you.

CASH: Erm . . . you may be right. But Branson is kind of a whole other thing. Mel Tillis's theatre is full almost every show, but that's because, a year in advance, his people go out and sign up these tour bus companies. I didn't have that going for me in Branson. The whole situation for me was disappointing, because it was *not* what I wanted to do with my life. I wanted to go out and perform for people and do something new. I didn't desert anybody and I don't think anybody deserted me. But Branson didn't work out for me and I won't ever go back.

HOSKYNS: You also closed the House of Cash [tourist attraction near Cash's home in Hendersonville, Tennessee] last year.

CASH: Yes. I don't wanna be in the tourist business. It was a collection of antiques and paraphernalia that June and I have gathered over the years, and it was very interesting to me [to watch] people to go through them, but we got tired of that. My mother died, for one thing [in 1991], and she was kind of the boss there.

HOSKYNS: The phenomenal sales of country music have finally reached a plateau after ten years. Do you think people are thirsting for something a little more soulful from Nashville?

CASH: There's a greater selection of songs now, but I think there's a glut of records that sound overproduced. A few people are trying to stylise their own music rather than sounding like the same hat acts over and over, and I think it'll mellow out to being real country music again. Some of the stations are startin' to play the veterans again. People like Haggard. George Jones gets a lot of play. Possibly they might play a track or two off this new album of mine, because it's a real country record in a lot of ways. It's got a country classic by Jimmie Rodgers, and then there's the Don Gibson song ["Sea of Heartbreak"] and "I Never Picked Cotton" [a 1970 hit for Roy Clark].

HOSKYNS: You transcend category, in any case. *American Recordings* was as much a folk album as a country album.

CASH: I've always loved folk music. It's the backbone of country, or it used to be. It's where country came from, and I think if country ever looks again to its roots and draws on that tradition it'll be in good shape.

HOSKYNS: Do you relate to people like Steve Earle and Dwight Yoakam as Nashville rebels? Earle's recent prison gig inevitably recalled your Folsom Prison and San Quentin albums.

CASH: Those two are my favourite country singers at the moment. Dwight's my friend. He went in and really told Columbia what he thought when they dropped me [in 1986]. I did a session with Steve Earle a year ago: we did a song called "In Your Mind" for *Dead Man Walking*. He's a lot like me back when I was younger. He wears his clothes from the inside out!

HOSKYNS: I heard that your next record with Rick Rubin will be a gospel album. It reminded me that when you first auditioned for Sam Phillips you described yourself as "a gospel singer."

CASH: Gospel music is so ingrained in my bones. I can't do a concert without singing a gospel song. It's the thing that inspired me as a child, growin' up on a cotton farm where work was drudgery. When I was in the field I sang gospel songs all the time, because they lifted me up above that black dirt.

HOSKYNS: Are there any songs you simply know you're going to have to do on the album?

CASH: Several we've already got recorded with just me and my guitar, but if we do any with a band, we've already got an arrangement for "Farther Along." Mike Campbell

[Heartbreakers guitarist] suggested that to me. There are others I love so much—some Sister Rosetta Tharpe songs. "Strange Things Happening Every Day," I gotta record that. And maybe "Didn't It Rain, Child." Plus the old *country* gospel things, like "How Beautiful Heaven Must Be."

HOSKYNS: Did you ever talk about gospel with Elvis?

CASH: Oh yes. That's *all* we talked about . . . well, we talked about girls, too! Elvis and I, a lot of shows we would sing together in the dressing room, and invariably we'd go to black gospel. In Tupelo, that was what he heard, and I was in Arkansas about 40 miles away. So we grew up on the same songs, everything from Bill Monroe to black gospel to the Chuck Wagon Gang. Elvis and Carl and I would sit in the dressing room before shows and sing those Blackwood Brothers gospel songs.

HOSKYNS: Some people would have it that when the Million Dollar Quartet [Presley, Cash, Carl Perkins and Jerry Lee Lewis] fortuitously came together at Sun, you actually went out shopping.

CASH: That is a tale RCA or somebody tried to get authenticated with a couple of people in Memphis—I guess to keep from having to deal with me on royalties. But the fact is, it was Carl's session and I was the first one there with him. Then Elvis walks in with his girlfriend, so the session stops. Elvis sits down at the piano, and then Jerry Lee Lewis comes in. I was all the way down at the other end of the piano from that big RCA mic, so you don't hear me. And when you do, I'm singin' real high, because I couldn't find my harmony.

HOSKYNS: Do you think you could ever have been a preacher?

CASH: No. I think in my world of religion you're *called* to preach or you don't preach. I've never been ordained to preach the Gospel.

HOSKYNS: What's your view of televangelists?

CASH: First of all, I don't know many of 'em, and I've made it a point not to know many of 'em. Because that kind of thing, if I was a preacher, that's definitely *not* what I would be doing. I would be preaching in a little country church somewhere, ministering to the spiritual needs of my little flock. And I don't think I would *ever* go on TV if I was a preacher. I'm not saying I don't condone that, but I don't support it. The only preacher who's been on TV that I like is Billy Graham, because I know him really well. His thing has never been money. We've sat together on the beach many an hour and he is what he appears to be.

HOSKYNS: Compared to someone like Jerry Lee Lewis, you seem to have done a little better at keeping the demons at bay.

CASH: I wish I had. I wish I had. They've eaten me alive a few times.

HOSKYNS: You've only been married twice, for one thing.

CASH: I never was one to change wives a lot. I love the one I've had now for the last 28 years. Boy, we've had a good time. It's been a party.

HOSKYNS: You're a man of apparent contradictions. A man who can record an album [*Bitter Tears*, 1964] about Native Americans on the one hand and a jingoistic anthem, "Sold Out of Flagpoles" [1976], on the other. Where does the truth lie?

CASH: I guess Kristofferson summed it up in the song he wrote about me: "He's a walking contradiction/Partly truth and partly fiction." And Patrick Carr [music writer] wrote in a story about me that I'm the Indian in the white man's camp. Maybe that's it, or maybe I'm the white man in the Indian's camp. I don't know. I'm here to live an interesting life, I'm not here to hurt the country establishment or any such thing. I pressured my producer to record *Bitter Tears*, and he almost fainted. Right now, looking back over the years, I think it's one of my two favourite albums that I ever recorded; the other one would be *Ride This Train* [1960]. A lot of Indians come to my shows and they like to feel that somebody in that other establishment cares for them. I'm still glad I was able to be the voice for them, for a few minutes anyway. All I've sung and talked about are the things you can find in the treaties the white man made with them in the first place. The songs don't ask for anything more than what's right for them.

HOSKYNS: On the eve of the presidential elections, how optimistic are you about America's future?

CASH: I'm very optimistic. I wish we'd stop meddling in little wars, though, or stop starting them. That bothers me. That *really* bothers me. It always has. I think we're messin' around in parts of the world where we don't belong. I think we should kind of mind of our own business, be a part of the UN but not try to jump ahead and lead it.

HOSKYNS: I have to ask this. Just how scared were you when you went into Folsom Prison in January 1968?

CASH: We weren't scared at all, but we went into a couple later that I was worried about getting out of. In 1980, we went to Vacaville in central California, and the concert was very coldly accepted. Afterwards we had to walk all the way across a field three or four hundred yards to get out. So I took June by the arm and we started to walk to the gate. And a bunch of convicts lined up across the entrance to the gate, as if to say, "You're not gettin' out." I thought, well, this is it, but I'm not gonna accept it till it happens. So I told June, just hold on and don't stop. And when I got right face to face with them, they backed off and let us through. I've only been to a couple of prisons since then.

HOSKYNS: How is the pain in your jaw these days?

CASH: It's pretty severe, almost all the time. Except when I'm onstage. I pray for that, and it works. It doesn't alter or hinder my performance. I don't take painkillers. I've got into trouble with them two or three times already.

HOSKYNS: How can you live with that pain?

CASH: After six, seven years you probably get to where you can handle it. Once I can get my face laid down on a soft pillow for about ten minutes, I can go off to sleep. I'm handling it. It's my pain. I'm not being brave—I'm not brave at all—but after what I've been through, I just know how to handle it.

HOSKYNS: You haven't sued? I thought everyone in America sued. [Cash's jaw was broken when a dental surgeon attempted to remove a cyst from it. Infection then set in, and "the hell started." He has so far had 34 surgical operations on his jaw.]

CASH: Everybody advised me to sue, but I wouldn't do it. I don't wanna do that with my life, I don't want that hassle.

HOSKYNS: The last song on *Unchained*, "I've Been Everywhere," could be your life story. Do you need to tour so much and work so hard?

CASH: For my soul, I do. My mother always told me that any talent is a gift from God and I always believed it. It's not that if you don't use it you lose it. I don't believe that. But if I quit, I would just live in front of the television and get fat and die. And I don't wanna do that.

HOSKYNS: There's an incredible work ethic in country music—people like Ernest Tubb touring till they drop.

CASH: Well, why not? People die in the workplace everywhere. You know, I just hope and pray I can die with my boots on— *really*. I've been in hospital beds, and I don't *wanna* end up there.

HOSKYNS: Do you never get tired of singing the same old songs?

CASH: Absolutely not. I got over that. I went through a period when I didn't wanna sing those old songs again, and I might have given 'em one or two in a show. But I finally decided that I was really cheatin' them *and* myself. And I started singin' all the old ones with *gusto* and *lust*, like I *love* them. And now, there's not a song they can ask me to do that I won't try, if I can remember the words to it. Those songs, they're part of me, an extension of me. When I get in front of a microphone, there's a part of me going through the mic to that audience, and they feel it and they know it if *I* feel it, and they'll turn it right back to me. And that's what performing is all about: sharing and communicating.

HOSKYNS: Do you see an American icon when you look in the mirror?

CASH: God, what a question! Shit! No. No. No. I see the pimples on my nose, and the fat jaw from the pain where it's swollen . . . thinning hair, whatever. Icon, no. Not in *my* mirror.

"I'M NOT A SINGER"

INTERVIEW BY TERRY GROSS
FRESH AIR
1997

TERRY GROSS: This is *Fresh Air*. I'm Terry Gross. Today we go into the archive to play back interviews with two music icons, Johnny Cash and Ray Charles. Our country may be politically divided, but on this Thanksgiving Day, I think we can all agree that their music is part of what has made America great. We'll start with Johnny Cash. I interviewed him in 1997 after the publication of his autobiography when he was sixty-five. He died in 2003.

He had his biggest hits in the fifties and sixties, songs like "Ring of Fire" and "I Walk the Line." As he said in his book, between the early seventies and early nineties, he didn't sell huge numbers of records, but he kept making music he was proud of. But in 1994, he teamed up with record producer Rick Rubin, who had produced many rap and rock hits. They recorded a series of albums without glossy studio production, focusing on songs they loved, including country songs, hymns, and covers of contemporary singer-songwriters.

As the autobiography says, the Cash and Rubin collaborations transformed Cash's image from Nashville has-been to hip icon. Let's begin with a song from that first collaboration. This is "Why Me, Lord?"

[*Sound bite of "Why Me, Lord?"*]

GROSS: Your career has, in many ways, been about both the sacred and the profane. You've always been Christian and have always sung hymns. And on the other hand, there were times in your life when, as you write in your book, when you'd been in and out of jails, hospitals, car wrecks, when you were a walking vision of death, and that's exactly how you felt, you say in your book.

Have you always been aware of that contradiction of, you know, the sacred and the profane running through your life?

JOHNNY CASH: Yeah, Kristofferson wrote a song, and in that song was a line that says—he wrote the song about me. He's—there's a—he's a walking contradiction, partly truth and partly fiction. And I've always explored various areas of society. And I love the young people. And I had an empathy for prisoners and did concerts for them back when I thought that it would make a difference—you know?—that they really were there to be rehabilitated.

GROSS: You grew up during the Depression. What are some of the things that your father did to make a living while you were a boy?

CASH: My father was a cotton farmer first and—but he didn't have any land or what land he had, he lost it in the Depression. So he worked as a woodman and cut pulpwood for the paper mills, rode the rails in boxcars going from one harvest to another to try to make a little money picking fruit or vegetables.

Did every kind of work imaginable from painting to shoveling to herding cattle. And he's always been such an inspiration to me because of the very kinds of things that he did and the kind of life he lived.

GROSS: You know, it's interesting that you say your father inspired you so much. I'm sure you wouldn't have wanted to lead his life picking cotton.

CASH: I did from—until I was eighteen years old, that is. Then I picked the guitar, and I've been picking it since.

GROSS: [*laughter*] Right. Did you have a plan to get out? Did you very much want to get out of the town where you were brought up and get out of picking cotton?

CASH: Yeah, I knew that when I left there at the age of eighteen, I wouldn't be back. And it was common knowledge among all the people there that when you graduate from high school here, you go to college or go get a job or something and do it on your own. And I haven't been unfamiliar with hard work. It was no problem for me. But first I hitchhiked to Pontiac, Michigan, and got a job working in Fisher Body making those 1951 Pontiacs.

I worked there three weeks, got really sick of it, went back home and joined the air force.

GROSS: You have such a wonderful, deep voice. Did you start singing before your voice changed?

CASH: Oh, yeah. I've got no deep voice today. I've got a cold. But when I was young, I had a high tenor voice. I used to sing Bill Monroe songs. And I'd sing Dennis Day songs like . . .

GROSS: Oh, no. [*laughter*]

CASH: Yeah, songs that he sang on the Jack Benny show.

GROSS: Wow.

CASH: Every week, he sang an old Irish folk song. And next day in the fields, I'd be singing that song if I was working in the fields. And I always loved those songs. And with my high tenor, I thought I was pretty good—you know?—almost as good as Dennis Day. But when I was seventeen—sixteen, my father and I cut wood all day long and I was swinging that crosscut saw and hauling wood.

And when I walked in the back door late that afternoon, I was singing [*singing*] "everybody going to have religion and glory, everybody going to be singing a story." I sang those old gospel songs for my mother, and she said, "Is that you?" And I said, "Yes, ma'am." And she came over and put her arms around me and said, "God's got his hands on you."

I still think of that, you know?

GROSS: She realized you had a gift.

CASH: That's what she said, yeah. She called it "the gift."

GROSS: So did you start singing different songs as your voice got deeper?

CASH: "Lucky Old Sun," "Memories Are Made of This," "16 Tons." I developed a pretty unusual style, I think. If I'm anything, I'm not a singer, but I'm a song stylist.

GROSS: What's the difference?

CASH: Well, I say I'm not a singer, so that means I can't sing. But—doesn't it? [*laughter*]

GROSS: Well, but, I mean, that's not true. I understand you're making a distinction, but you certainly can sing. Yeah, go ahead.

CASH: Thank you. Well, a song stylist is, like, to take an old folk song like "Delia's Gone" and do a modern white man's version of it. A lot of those I did that way, you know? I would take songs that I'd loved as a child and redo them in my mind for the new voice I had, the low voice.

GROSS: I know that you briefly took singing lessons. And you say in your new book that your singing teacher told you, you know, don't let anybody change your voice. Don't even bother with the singing lessons. How did you end up taking lessons in the first place?

CASH: My mother did that. And she was determined that I was going to leave the farm and do well in life. And she thought with the gift, I might be able to do that. So she took in washing. She got a washing machine in 1942 as soon as we got electricity and she took in washing. She washed the schoolteacher's clothes and anybody she could and sent me for singing lessons for three dollars per lesson.

And that's how she made the money to send me.

GROSS: When you got to Memphis, Elvis Presley had already recorded "That's All Right." Sam Phillips had produced him for his label Sun Records. You called Sam Phillips and asked for an audition. Did it take a lot of nerve to make that phone call?

CASH: No, it just took the right time. I was fully confident that I was going to see Sam Phillips and to record for him that when I called him, I thought, I'm going to get on Sun Records. So I called him and he turned me down flat. Then two weeks later, I got turned down again. He told me over the phone that he couldn't sell gospel music so—as it was independent, not a lot of money, you know?

So I didn't press that issue. But one day, I just decided I'm ready to go. So I went down with my guitar and sat on the front steps of his recording studio. I met him when he came in and I said, "I'm John Cash. I'm the one who's been calling. And if you'd listen to me, I believe you'll be glad you did." And he said, "Come on in." That was a good lesson for me, you know, to believe in myself.

GROSS: So what did Phillips actually respond to most, of the songs that you played him?

CASH: He responded most to a song of mine called, "Hey Porter," which was on the first record. But he asked me to go write a love song, or maybe a bitter weeper. So I wrote a song called "Cry, Cry, Cry," went back in, and recorded that for the other side of the record.

GROSS: I want to play what I think was your first big hit, "I Walk the Line."

CASH: That was my third record.

GROSS: And you wrote this song. Tell me the story of how you wrote it. What you were thinking about at the time?

CASH: In the air force, I had an old Wilcox-Gay recorder, and I used to hear guitar runs on that recorder going [*vocalizing*] like the chords on "I Walk the Line." And I always wanted to write a love song using that theme, you know, that tune. And so I started to write the song. And I was in Gladewater, Texas, one night with Carl Perkins and I said, "I've got a good idea for a song." And I sang him the first verse that I had written, and I said it's called "Because You're Mine." And he said, "'I Walk the Line' is a better title." So I changed it to "I Walk the Line."

GROSS: Now, were you thinking of your own life when you wrote this?

CASH: It was kind of a prodding myself to play it straight, Johnny.

GROSS: And was this—I think I read that this was supposed to be a ballad. I mean, it was supposed to be slow when you first wrote it.

CASH: That's the way I sang it, yeah, at first. But Sam wanted it up—you know, up-tempo. And I put paper in the strings of my guitar to get that [*vocalizing*] sound, and with the bass and the lead guitar, there it was. Bare and stark, that song was, when it was released. And I heard it on the radio and I really didn't like it, and I called Sam Phillips and asked him please not to send out any more records of that song.

GROSS: Why?

CASH: He laughed at me. I just didn't like the way it sounded to me. I didn't know I sounded that way. And I didn't like it. I don't know. But he said let's give it a chance, and it was just a few days until—that's all it took to take off.

[*Sound bite of "I Walk the Line"*]

GROSS: I think it was in the late 1950s that you started doing prison concerts, which you eventually became very famous for. What got you started performing in prison?

CASH: Well, I had a song called "Folsom Prison Blues" that was a hit just before "I Walk the Line." And the people in Texas heard about it at the state prison and got to writing me letters asking me to come down there. So I responded and then the warden called me and asked if I would come down and do a show for the prisoners in Texas.

And so we went down and there's a rodeo at all these shows that the prisoners have there. And in between the rodeo things, they asked me to set up and do two or three songs. So that was what I did. I did "Folsom Prison Blues," which they thought was their song—you know?—and "I Walk the Line," "Hey Porter," "Cry, Cry, Cry." And then the word got around on the grapevine that Johnny Cash is all right and that you ought to see him.

So the requests started coming in from other prisoners all over the United States. And then the word got around. So I always wanted to record that, you know, to record a show because of the reaction I got. It was far and above anything I had ever had in my life, the complete explosion of noise and reaction that they gave me with every song. So then I came back the next year and played the prison again, the New Year's Day show, came back again a third year and did the show.

And then I kept talking to my producers at Columbia about recording one of those shows. So we went into Folsom on February 11, 1968, and recorded a show live.

GROSS: Well, why don't we hear "Folsom Prison Blues" from your live "At Folsom Prison" record? This is Johnny Cash.

[*Sound bite of "Folsom Prison Blues, Live"*]

GROSS: I guess Merle Haggard was in the audience for one of your San Quentin concerts. It must have been pretty exciting to find that out. That was before he . . .

CASH: Yeah.

GROSS: . . . had recorded, I think, that he was in there.

CASH: Yeah, ['59] and ['60], right on the front row was Merle Haggard.

GROSS: Yeah, and who knew?

CASH: I mean, I didn't know that until about 1963, '62. And he told me all about it. He saw every show that I did there. And, of course, the rest is history for Merle. He came out and immediately had success himself.

GROSS: A few years ago, you started making records with Rick Rubin. Tell me how you and he first met up. It seemed initially like a very improbable match. He had produced a lot of rap records and produced the Beastie Boys and the Red Hot Chili Peppers. You know, it would seem like a surprising match. It ended up being a fantastic match. How did he approach you?

CASH: Well, my contract with Mercury PolyGram Nashville was about to expire. And I never had really been happy. The company, the record company, just didn't put any promotion behind me. I think one album, maybe the last one I did, they pressed five hundred copies. And I was just disgusted with it. And about that time that I got to feeling that way, Lou Robin, my manager, came to me and talked to me about a man called Rick Rubin that he had been talking to that wanted me to sign with his record company.

That was American Recordings. I said, "I like the name, maybe it'd be OK." So I said, "I'd like to meet the guy. I'd like for him to tell me what he can do with me that they're not doing now." So he came to my concert in Orange County, California, I believe this was like, ['93] when he first came and listened to the show. And then afterwards, I went in the dressing room and sat and talked to him.

And, you know, he had his hair—I don't think it's ever been cut and very—dresses like a hobo, usually—clean but . . . [*laughter*] Was the kind of guy I really felt comfortable with, actually. I think I was more comfortable with him than I would have been with a producer with a suit on. What I said, "What are you going to do with me that nobody else has been able to do to sell records with me?"

And he said, "Well, I don't know that we will sell records." He said, "I would like you to go with me and sit in my living room with a guitar and two microphones and just sing to your heart's content everything you ever wanted to record." I said, "That sounds good to me." So I did that. And day after day, three weeks, I sang for him.

And when I finally stopped, he had been saying, like, the last day or so, he'd been saying, now, I think we should put this one in the album. So without him saying I want to record you and release an album, he kept—he started saying, let's put this one in the album. So the album, this big question, you know, began to take form, take shape. And Rick and I would weed out the songs.

There were songs that didn't feel good to us that we would say let's don't consider that one. And then we'd focus on the ones that we did like, that felt right and sounded right. And if I didn't like the performance on that song, I would keep trying it and do take after take until it felt comfortable with me and felt that it was coming out of me and my guitar and my voice as one, that it was right for my soul.

That's how I felt about all those things in that first album. And I got really excited about it. But then we went into the studio and tried to record some with different musicians, and it didn't sound good. It didn't work. So we put together the album with just a guitar and myself.

GROSS: Yeah, I was really glad you did it that way. There's something just so—just emotionally naked.

CASH: Yeah.

GROSS: And there's so much emotion in your voice. And it just all, you know, comes across really clearly.

CASH: Thank you.

GROSS: Johnny Cash, I want to thank you so much for talking with us.

CASH: I want to say, you're really good at what you do. And I appreciate you. Thank you.

THE LAST INTERVIEW

INTERVIEW BY KURT LODER
MTV
2003

LODER: Well, you've been a star forever, and you're still as big a star as you've ever been; you've got these six Video Music Award nominations. How do you feel about that?

CASH: Kinda overwhelmed. I'm very grateful for the nominations and for all the votes.

LODER: Do you enjoy the video process; do you like to make videos?

CASH: Not especially, no. Not especially.

LODER: Why not?

CASH: Well, I don't know. [*Loder chuckles*] It's uh, it's just work. Sometimes it's really fun like, I like to—I enjoyed doing the "Hurt" video. I enjoyed doing that very much because I felt we were doing something worthwhile. That it was something that was kind of special.

LODER: It's a very emotional video. I mean, did you feel very emotional doing it?

CASH: I did; I did. I felt very emotional doing the "Hurt" video, yes.

LODER: Where did the song come from; did Rick Rubin play it for you and say, "We're gonna do this song?"

CASH: Yeah.

LODER: What did you think when you first heard it?

CASH: Yeah, Rick played the song for me, and I uh [*pause*] when I heard the record, I said, "I can't do that song, it's not my style. It just—" He said, "Well let's try it another way; let me do something." So he put down a track and I listened to it, so we started working on that—from there we started working until we got the record made.

LODER: How did he come to—how did he approach you to be on his label?

CASH: I was doing a show in California, and um, when I came offstage, my manager Lou Robin came to me and said, "There's a man here named Rick Rubin that said he would like to meet you, that has a record company, and he would like to record you." And I said, "I don't wanna meet him." And he said, "Yeah? I think you might like him." I said, "Why?" And he said, "Well, he's different; he's not like the rest of them."

LODER: So true.

CASH: And uh, so, I told him, "Bring him back," and so, I went back, and there's Rick, and immediately I liked him, and I said, "So if you had me on your record label, what would you do that nobody else has done?" And he said, "What I would do is let you sit down before a microphone with your guitar and sing every song you want to record. [*Loder chuckles*] Just you and your guitar." And I said, "You're talking about a dream I had a long time ago, to do an album called 'Late and Alone,'" and he said, "That's it; that's the kind of record that we want to make." Well, that was my first American record.

LODER: And looking back at all that you've done, do you have any regrets about what you've done, or do you think it's—I mean, there's so much you've accomplished.

CASH: I used to, but I don't—I forgave myself. When God forgave me, I figured I'd better do it, too. So, uh, everything's all right now.

LODER: Going back to songs like "Folsom Prison Blues," and that's about shooting somebody, and some of your songs are about God, love, and murder. Did people criticize you for that sort of song back in those years?

CASH: Always have; they always have. I've always had that pointed up in my face that I wrote a song with a line in it, that "I shot a man in Reno just to watch him die." But, you know, I wasn't the first. In the late twenties, country singer Jimmy Rogers, in one of his Blue Yodel songs, had a line that says, "I'm gonna shoot poor Thelma, just to see her jump and fall." [*Loder chuckles. Cash chuckles, too*] He may have been the first to write a line like that, I don't know, but I wasn't thinking of Jimmy when I wrote it, I was thinking that I was in that prison. That's where I try to—I try to put myself in the place that I'm singing about. You can't let people delegate to you what you should do when it's coming from way in here, [*points to his chest*] you know? Somebody comes up in your face with somethin', tells you what you oughta do. Then, uh, you can take them at their word or you can just turn your back, you know. I wouldn't let anybody influence me into thinking I was doing the wrong thing by singing about death, hell, and drugs. 'Cause I've always done that, and I always will.

LODER: You were married for more than thirty years. What's the secret to that; how do people stay together that long?

CASH: We were together forty years; we worked on the road together since 1963, and we got married in '68. And, uh, the secret for a happy marriage? Separate bathrooms.

LODER: [*laughs*] Really, that's it?

CASH: I think so. [*chuckles*]

LODER: When June passed on, did she have any advice for you; did she say keep going, keep making music, or . . .

CASH: Oh, she always said that. Oh, yeah. She was my great encourager. She loved the "Hurt" video. She loved it. And I'm so glad she lived long enough to see it do what it did and to get the attention that it got, because she did love the "Hurt" video. And, uh, she was my biggest critic, too. If she didn't like something that I did, she told me about it in a hot minute. [*Loder laughs*]

LODER: I imagine it must be—to be married so long, and to lose someone, I imagine people would sometimes just want to stop and say—you know, 'cause spouses, sometimes, just follow each other, but you're still going and ready to go. Where do you get the energy—the strength—

CASH: She told me in the hospital, said, "Go to work." I said, "What're you talking about?" She said, "Don't worry about me; go to work." And at the funeral, I could almost hear her saying, "Go to work." Three days after the funeral—everybody said you're crazy—but three days after the funeral, I was in the studio.

LODER: Really.

CASH: Yeah. And I stayed in the studio for two weeks. And it was great therapy for me, and I think I accomplished more in that couple of weeks than in most of the other year combined.

LODER: How much has record making changed—well, it's changed a lot, I'm sure, since you were at Sun Studios—is it, just, way out of control, now? Is it just too big?

CASH: Oh, no, it's easier; it's easier. With all the new technology, it's great. With the Pro Tools, and all that. [*Loder laughs*]

LODER: I wonder how you, when you look back at what

you've done, do you realize this monumental amount of work you've created and what it means in American music—do you feel like you're a monument of American music, or do you just look at yourself as John Cash?

CASH: Just as John Cash.

LODER: You must know how people feel about you, right? Do you hear from a lot of fans all the time?

CASH: Yeah, quite often, uh-huh. I hear from a lot of fans, yeah. I do. [*pause*] Look, I appreciate all that, all the—all the praise and the glory, but, uh, but it doesn't change the way I feel about anything, really. I just do what I do, and just hope that people enjoy it, and just try to be myself in whatever I do.

LODER: I've talked to a lot of younger musicians—Kid Rock, and Bono from U2—you have so many fans among musicians, I mean, do you get to meet them, or do they write to you or call you?

CASH: Oh, yeah. Yeah, I get to meet them. I talk to Bono quite often—I haven't—I've never met Kid Rock yet; I'm looking forward to—my little world has been kind of limited, you know, lately, since June's death, I've, uh, kind of hung close to home, here.

LODER: You were there at the beginning of rock 'n' roll music; do you still keep in touch, like, Jerry Lee Lewis, do you hear from any of these people—

CASH: I haven't heard from The Killer in, uh, quite a while. I get an invitation to his birthday party every year. I haven't heard from him in quite a while. I understand he's doing well. Glad to hear that. I love The Killer. We're good friends.

LODER: Do you remember touring with those people, [*unintelligible*]?

CASH: Oh, yes. I toured with him. There was a package of myself, Jerry Lee, Roy Orbison, and Carl Perkins.

LODER: Wow.

CASH: We toured all over the United States and Canada.

LODER: So, you're out on the road in the early days with Jerry Lee and all these people and it was crazy—pretty crazy times?

CASH: We were all young and wild and crazy.

LODER: How crazy were you?

CASH: I was crazy as you can get. I mean, crazy, crazy. Yeah. At the time we were doing these tours, we discovered amphetamines. Or I did, anyway. [*Loder chuckles*] And, um, [*pause*] Jerry was, uh, you know, he, uh, he thought he was going to hell for not preaching. He went to seminary, and he wanted to be a preacher, but he turned to rock and roll, and he'd tell all of us—he'd go into a tangent some night backstage, and tell us how we're going to hell for singing the kind of music we're singing. I said, "Maybe you're right, Killer. Maybe you are. Maybe you're right. I don't know. I don't know."

LODER: I wanted to ask you, I think, uh, people that have no faith probably look at death as something very scary, but you believe, and you have faith, I mean, does it make it easier to look ahead and say, "Well, my life may end, but it's been good; I'm not afraid."

CASH: Oh, I expect my life to end pretty soon; you know, I'm seventy-one years old. And, um, I have great faith, though. I have unshakeable faith; I've never been angry with God. I've never been—uh, I've never turned by back on God, so to speak. I never thought that God wasn't there. That, uh—I knew that He is my counselor; He is my wisdom. All the good things in my life come from Him.

LODER: Where do you think we go, afterwards?

CASH: Where do we go? When we die, you mean? Oh. Well, we all hope to go to Heaven.

JOHNNY CASH (1932–2003) was a singer, songwriter, and giant of the American country music industry. Born to a poor cotton-farming family in Arkansas, Cash began his musical career after serving in the military in the early 1950s. His songs, including "Folsom Prison Blues" and "I Walk the Line," have remained country music standards. He is one of the best-selling musicians of all time and is one of the few artists to be inducted in the Country Music, Rock & Roll, and Gospel Music Halls of Fame.

PETER GURALNICK has been called "a national resource" by critic Nat Hentoff for work that has argued passionately and persuasively for the vitality of this country's intertwined black and white musical traditions. His books include the prize-winning, two-volume biography of Elvis Presley, *Last Train to Memphis* and *Careless Love; Searching for Robert Johnson; Sweet Soul Music*; and *Dream Boogie: The Triumph of Sam Cooke*. His 2015 biography, *Sam Phillips: The Man Who Invented Rock 'n' Roll*, was a finalist for the Plutarch Award for Best Biography of the Year, awarded by the Biographers International Organization. His most recent book is *Looking to Get Lost: Adventures in Music and Writing*.

PETE SEEGER (1919–2014) was an American folk singer and prominent social activist. After dropping out of Harvard in 1938, he joined the Almanac Singers and the Weavers, and collaborated closely with Woody Guthrie, Joan Baez, and other musicians. Seeger often infused his music with his counterculture political beliefs, and many of his songs, including "Where Have All the Flowers Gone?" and "Turn! Turn! Turn!" have endured as cornerstones of American protest movements.

JUNE CARTER CASH (1929–2003) was a Grammy Award–winning country singer, songwriter, and actress. A member of the Carter Trio along with her sisters, a fixture at the Grand Ole Opry, and a student of director Lee Strasberg, she was best known for her musical collaborations with her husband Johnny Cash, whom she married in 1968. Carter received widespread praise for her popularization of folk staples like "Jackson" and "Wildwood Flower," and for writing Cash's "Ring of Fire."

PATRICK CARR is a veteran music journalist known for his contributions to *Country Music* magazine, *The Village Voice*, and *Slate*. Carr befriended Johnny Cash beginning in the 1990s and was the coauthor of Cash's second autobiography in 1997. He is also the editor of *The Illustrated History of Country Music*.

GLENN JORGENSON is a sober-living advocate and businessman based in South Dakota. In 1970, he helped establish a chemical dependency program at River Park in Pierre, South Dakota. He is best known for his television show *It's Great to Be Alive*, which aired throughout the Midwest and featured interviews with celebrities on alcoholism and other substance addictions. He continues to run the River Park Foundation with his wife, Phyllis.

BARNEY HOSKYNS is a British journalist and cofounder of the online music journalism archive *Rock's Backpages*. He is also the former contributing editor of British *Vogue*, where he covered musicians, pop culture, and music history. He has written for *Harper's Bazaar*, *Spin Magazine*, and *Rolling Stone*, and is the author of the book *Glam! Bowie, Bolan & the Glitter Rock Revolution* and the memoir *Never Enough: A Way Through Addiction*.

TERRY GROSS is the host and executive producer of *Fresh Air* from WHYY-FM in Philadelphia and NPR. She has interviewed politicians, artists, musicians, professors, and other notable figures throughout her forty-five-year career in the American radio broadcast industry. She is the recipient of a Peabody Award, an Edward R. Murrow Award, and a National Humanities Medal, and is an inductee of the Radio Hall of Fame.

KURT LODER is a journalist, music and film critic, and television personality best known for his work with MTV News. He is a former editor of *Circus* magazine and contributor to *Rolling Stone*, and currently hosts the talk show *True Stories* on Sirius XM. He became famous for hosting *This Week in Rock* on MTV beginning in 1987.

THE LAST INTERVIEW SERIES

FRED ROGERS: THE LAST INTERVIEW AND OTHER CONVERSATIONS

"I think one of the greatest gifts you can give anybody is the gift of your honest self."

$16.99 / $21.99 CAN
978-1-61219-895-8
ebook: 978-1-61219-896-5

SHIRLEY CHISHOLM: THE LAST INTERVIEW AND OTHER CONVERSATIONS

"All I can say is that I'm a shaker-upper. That's exactly what I am.

$16.99 / $21.99 CAN
978-1-61219-897-2
ebook: 978-1-61219-898-9

RUTH BADER GINSBURG : THE LAST INTERVIEW AND OTHER CONVERSATIONS

"No one ever expected me to go to law school. I was supposed to be a high school teacher, or how else could I earn a living?"

$17.99 / $22.99 CAN
978-1-61219-919-1
ebook: 978-1-61219-920-7

THE LAST INTERVIEW SERIES

MARILYN MONROE: THE LAST INTERVIEW AND OTHER CONVERSATIONS

"I'm so many people. They shock me sometimes.
I wish I was just me!"

$16.99 / $21.99 CAN
978-1-61219-877-4
ebook: 978-1-61219-878-1

FRIDA KAHLO: THE LAST INTERVIEW AND OTHER CONVERSATIONS

"The only thing I know is that I paint because I need to, and I paint always whatever passes through my head, without any other consideration."

$16.99 / $21.99 CAN
978-1-61219-875-0
ebook: 978-1-61219-876-7

TONI MORRISON: THE LAST INTERVIEW AND OTHER CONVERSATIONS

"Knowledge is what's important, you know?
Not the erasure, but the confrontation of it."

$16.99 / 21.99 CAN
978-1-61219-873-6
ebook: 978-1-61219-874-3

THE LAST INTERVIEW SERIES

GRAHAM GREENE: THE LAST INTERVIEW AND OTHER CONVERSATIONS

"I think to exclude politics from a novel is to exclude a whole aspect of life."

$16.99 / 21.99 CAN
978-1-61219-814-9
ebook: 978-1-61219-815-6

ANTHONY BOURDAIN: THE LAST INTERVIEW AND OTHER CONVERSATIONS

"We should feed our enemies Chicken McNuggets."

$16.99 / $21.99 CAN
978-1-61219-824-8
ebook: 978-1-61219-825-5

URSULA K. LE GUIN: THE LAST INTERVIEW AND OTHER CONVERSATIONS

"Resistance and change often begin in art. Very often in our art, the art of words."

$16.99 / $21.99 CAN
978-1-61219-779-1
ebook: 978-1-61219-780-7

THE LAST INTERVIEW SERIES

PRINCE: THE LAST INTERVIEW
AND OTHER CONVERSATIONS

"That's what you want. Transcendence.
When that happens—oh, boy."

$16.99 / $22.99 CAN
978-1-61219-745-6
ebook: 978-1-61219-746-3

JULIA CHILD: THE LAST INTERVIEW
AND OTHER CONVERSATIONS

"I'm not a chef, I'm a teacher and a cook."

$16.99 / $22.99 CAN
978-1-61219-733-3
ebook: 978-1-61219-734-0

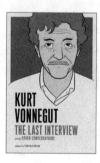

KURT VONNEGUT: THE LAST INTERVIEW

"I think it can be tremendously refreshing if a creator
of literature has something on his mind other than
the history of literature so far. Literature should not
disappear up its own asshole, so to speak."

$15.95 / $17.95 CAN
978-1-61219-090-7
ebook: 978-1-61219-091-4

THE LAST INTERVIEW SERIES

JACQUES DERRIDA: THE LAST INTERVIEW
LEARNING TO LIVE FINALLY

"I am at war with myself, it's true, you couldn't possibly know to what extent... I say contradictory things that are, we might say, in real tension; they are what construct me, make me live, and will make me die."

translated by PASCAL-ANNE BRAULT and MICHAEL NAAS

$15.95 / $17.95 CAN
978-1-61219-094-5
ebook: 978-1-61219-032-7

ROBERTO BOLAÑO: THE LAST INTERVIEW

"Posthumous: It sounds like the name of a Roman gladiator, an unconquered gladiator. At least that's what poor Posthumous would like to believe. It gives him courage."

translated by SYBIL PEREZ and others

$15.95 / $17.95 CAN
978-1-61219-095-2
ebook: 978-1-61219-033-4

JORGE LUIS BORGES: THE LAST INTERVIEW

"Believe me: the benefits of blindness have been greatly exaggerated. If I could see, I would never leave the house, I'd stay indoors reading the many books that surround me."

translated by KIT MAUDE

$15.95 / $15.95 CAN
978-1-61219-204-8
ebook: 978-1-61219-205-5

THE LAST INTERVIEW SERIES

HANNAH ARENDT: THE LAST INTERVIEW

"There are no dangerous thoughts for the simple reason that thinking itself is such a dangerous enterprise."

$15.95 / $15.95 CAN
978-1-61219-311-3
ebook: 978-1-61219-312-0

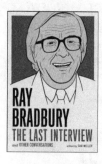

RAY BRADBURY: THE LAST INTERVIEW

"You don't have to destroy books to destroy a culture. Just get people to stop reading them."

$15.95 / $15.95 CAN
978-1-61219-421-9
ebook: 978-1-61219-422-6

JAMES BALDWIN: THE LAST INTERVIEW

"You don't realize that you're intelligent until it gets you into trouble."

$15.95 / $15.95 CAN
978-1-61219-400-4
ebook: 978-1-61219-401-1

THE LAST INTERVIEW SERIES

GABRIEL GÁRCIA MÁRQUEZ: THE LAST INTERVIEW

"The only thing the Nobel Prize is good for is not having to wait in line."

$15.95 / $15.95 CAN
978-1-61219-480-6
ebook: 978-1-61219-481-3

LOU REED: THE LAST INTERVIEW

"Hubert Selby. William Burroughs. Allen Ginsberg. Delmore Schwartz... I thought if you could do what those writers did and put it to drums and guitar, you'd have the greatest thing on earth."

$15.95 / $15.95 CAN
978-1-61219-478-3
ebook: 978-1-61219-479-0

ERNEST HEMINGWAY: THE LAST INTERVIEW

"The most essential gift for a good writer is a built-in, shockproof shit detector."

$15.95 / $20.95 CAN
978-1-61219-522-3
ebook: 978-1-61219-523-0

THE LAST INTERVIEW SERIES

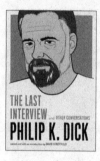

PHILIP K. DICK: THE LAST INTERVIEW

"The basic thing is, how frightened are you of chaos? And how happy are you with order?"

$15.95 / $20.95 CAN
978-1-61219-526-1
ebook: 978-1-61219-527-8

NORA EPHRON: THE LAST INTERVIEW

"You better *make* them care about what you think. It had better be quirky or perverse or thoughtful enough so that you hit some chord in them. Otherwise, it doesn't work."

$15.95 / $20.95 CAN
978-1-61219-524-7
ebook: 978-1-61219-525-4

JANE JACOBS: THE LAST INTERVIEW

"I would like it to be understood that all our human economic achievements have been done by ordinary people, not by exceptionally educated people, or by elites, or by supernatural forces."

$15.95 / $20.95 CAN
978-1-61219-534-6
ebook: 978-1-61219-535-3

THE LAST INTERVIEW SERIES

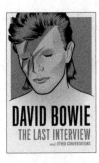

DAVID BOWIE: THE LAST INTERVIEW

"I have no time for glamour. It seems a ridiculous thing to strive for ... A clean pair of shoes should serve quite well."

$16.99 / $22.99 CAN
978-1-61219-575-9
ebook: 978-1-61219-576-6

MARTIN LUTHER KING, JR.: THE LAST INTERVIEW

"Injustice anywhere is a threat to justice everywhere."

$15.99 / $21.99 CAN
978-1-61219-616-9
ebook: 978-1-61219-617-6

CHRISTOPHER HITCHENS: THE LAST INTERVIEW

"If someone says I'm doing this out of faith, I say, Why don't you do it out of conviction?"

$15.99 / $20.99 CAN
978-1-61219-672-5
ebook: 978-1-61219-673-2

THE LAST INTERVIEW SERIES

BILLIE HOLIDAY: THE LAST INTERVIEW AND OTHER CONVERSATIONS

"What comes out is what I feel. I hate straight singing."

$16.99 / $21.99 CAN
978-1-61219-674-9
ebook: 978-1-61219-675-6

HUNTER S. THOMPSON: THE LAST INTERVIEW

"I feel in the mood to write a long weird story—a tale so strange and terrible that it will change the brain of the normal reader forever."

$15.99 / $20.99 CAN
978-1-61219-693-0
ebook: 978-1-61219-694-7

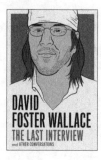

DAVID FOSTER WALLACE: THE LAST INTERVIEW AND OTHER CONVERSATIONS

"I'm a typical American. Half of me is dying to give myself away, and the other half is continually rebelling."

$16.99 / 21.99 CAN
978-1-61219-741-8
ebook: 978-1-61219-742-5